Henry Charles Banister

Lectures on Musical Analysis,

Delivered Before the Royal Normal College and Academy of Music for the Blind.

Second Edition

Henry Charles Banister

Lectures on Musical Analysis,
Delivered Before the Royal Normal College and Academy of Music for the Blind. Second Edition

ISBN/EAN: 9783337071769

Printed in Europe, USA, Canada, Australia, Japan

Cover: Foto ©Thomas Meinert / pixelio.de

More available books at **www.hansebooks.com**

LECTURES

ON

MUSICAL ANALYSIS,

DELIVERED BEFORE THE

ROYAL NORMAL COLLEGE AND ACADEMY OF
MUSIC FOR THE BLIND.

BY

HENRY C. BANISTER,

PROFESSOR OF HARMONY, COUNTERPOINT AND COMPOSITION (AND OF THE
PIANOFORTE) IN THAT INSTITUTION, IN THE GUILDHALL SCHOOL
OF MUSIC, AND IN THE ROYAL ACADEMY OF MUSIC.

Second edition revised.

LONDON:
GEORGE BELL & SONS, YORK STREET,
COVENT GARDEN.
1888.

TO
FRANCIS JOESPH CAMPBELL, Esq., LL.D., F.R.G.S.,

I Dedicate this Volume,

BOTH AS A TESTIMONY OF PERSONAL FRIENDSHIP,

AND IN RECOGNITION OF THE ENCOURAGING INTEREST

TAKEN BY HIM IN THE

DELIVERY OF THE LECTURES HEREIN CONTAINED AT THE

COLLEGE WHICH HE DIRECTS WITH SO MUCH ACTIVE ENERGY

AND WITH SUCH ADMINISTRATIVE ABILITY.

H. C. B.

PREFACE.

It has been my custom for some years past, in my capacity as Professor of Harmony, Counterpoint, and Composition at the Royal Normal College and Academy of Music for the Blind, Upper Norwood, to assemble the Pupils in the evening, after a day's class-work, in the hall of the College, once a fortnight, to listen to a Lecture upon the structure of Musical Compositions, illustrated upon the Pianoforte. This seems to me to be the kind of training which is of great importance to all Musical Students, as an adjunct to their own theoretical studies and exercise work. In the case of the specially circumstanced audience of young people whom I had the pleasure of addressing, it was an experiment that I made, not without some misgiving as to my power of making the subject clear and interesting to those who could not scan the works analysed, or trace in the copy the course of the exposition offered ; although the training in the College includes frequent performances in their hearing of the entire *répertoire* of the finest Pianoforte music, with brief explanations. All doubt was over, however, after the first attempt. The interest awakened by the first Lecture was evinced unmistakably, both at the time and afterwards, throughout the College, by conversation and discussion. That interest has never flagged ; which has testified to the charm of the subject, and to the excellent mental training which the Pupils receive in the admirable Institution in which they are educated.

The continued eagerness among the younger as well as the elder students, led me to consider whether, if the Lectures, originally delivered from rough notes, were fairly arranged in readable form, they might be useful to Musical Students generally; and I determined to make a selection from those delivered, and so to prepare them for the press. This volume is the result. It is offered, not as by any means furnishing a complete course of instruction in Musical Analysis. This would require a much larger work. But, in familiar manner, it deals consecutively with some of those elementary principles of Musical Structure, illustrated in the works of the Great Masters, with which every student should become acquainted, who aspires to intelligence about the Art. Movement Structure is the one subject herein expatiated upon. The work is not a treatise upon the art of Composition, but a commentary upon existing compositions, and an explanation of various structures. I have not attempted completeness, fulness, or didactic dogmatism. I have adhered to the general familiar colloquialism which all along has characterized my "talks" with my blind pupils: for "are you going to *talk* to us to-night?" has been the form of inquiry: the formal term *Lecture* has been little used.

Let these familiar papers, then, be accepted as a sample of the kind of work which is being carried on in the Institution; and further, of the kind of helpful work which, without any great pretension, any friendly teacher may carry on with willing pupils. And, still further, let Musical Students accept these Lectures as affording some helpful guidance in their analytical studies: showing them what to look for, and how to look for it.

It will be evident that, whereas I had the opportunity when delivering the Lectures of playing the illustrative passages from the works analysed, reiterating them, and showing their contextual and other bearings, I have been compelled in this volume, by considerations of space, to give only just such brief extracts as are absolutely necessary to render the analysis at all intelligible, and to enable a reader to follow the explanations. But as so large a proportion of the works referred to are within reach, and should be in possession of every earnest Musical Student, I strongly urge that this book be read and studied with the works quoted also before the eye, so that all the references may be made, and the complete passages examined, from which brief extracts only are here given; as well as the entire Movements in which those passages occur. These entire Movements were in most cases played by me, in connection with the delivery of the Lectures.

The identification of the Sonatas of Beethoven is by the *Opus* numbers. Those of Haydn and Mozart being differently numbered in various editions, it will be convenient here to state that the numbers herein given are those in Pauer's edition, published by Augener and Co.

After most of these Lectures had been delivered, and some were already in type, I had the privilege of hearing Professor Sir G. A. Macfarren lecture on some of the Sonatas by Beethoven, and was gratified to find some of the analytical remarks made by myself confirmed by the coincidence of so high an authority.

I have the pleasure of acknowledging the courtesy of Mr. Swinburne in readily according me permission to grace my pages by inserting the two exquisite *Roundels* quoted in the eighth and eleventh Lectures.

H. C. B.

London, March 1887.

CONTENTS.

LECTURE I.
INTRODUCTION. ANALYSIS DEFINED. THE SONATA, SYMPHONY, ETC. FIRST MOVEMENT FORM: FIRST SUBJECT: GENERAL CHARACTERISTICS 1

LECTURE II.
FIRST MOVEMENTS, *continued*: SECOND SUBJECT. CONNECTING PASSAGES 13

LECTURE III.
FIRST MOVEMENTS, *continued*: SECOND SUBJECT IN OTHER KEYS THAN THE DOMINANT. MOVEMENTS IN THE MINOR MODE 39

LECTURE IV.
MOVEMENTS IN THE MINOR MODE, *continued* 69

LECTURE V.
INTRODUCTIONS TO MOVEMENTS 95

LECTURE VI.
SECOND PART, OR FREE FANTASIA 115

LECTURE VII.
SECOND PART, *continued* 135

LECTURE VIII.

SECOND PART, *continued*: SUMMARY 169

LECTURE IX.

MOVEMENT OF EPISODE. RONDO. EARLY EXAMPLES. RAMEAU, COUPERIN, BACH 205

LECTURE X.

THE RONDO, *continued*: HAYDN AND MOZART ... 227

LECTURE XI.

THE RONDO, *continued*: EXTENSION: CONJUNCTION WITH FIRST MOVEMENT FORM. DUSSEK, BEETHOVEN, WEBER, MENDELSSOHN, BENNETT, ETC. GENERAL REQUIREMENTS IN STRUCTURE 253

LECTURE XII.

THE CODA AND CODETTA 271

LECTURE XIII.

THE MINUET AND SCHERZO 287

LECTURE XIV.

FUGUE 311

LECTURE XV.

FUGUE, *continued* 339

LECTURE XVI.

GENERAL SUMMARY. EXCEPTIONAL STRUCTURES. THE FANTASIA. THE CONCERTO. THE OVERTURE. AIRS WITH VARIATIONS. VOCAL MUSIC. CONCLUSION ... 361

INDEX 371

LECTURES ON MUSICAL ANALYSIS.

LECTURE I.

MUSICAL ANALYSIS DEFINED. A MOVEMENT. SONATA, OR FIRST-MOVEMENT FORM: MOVEMENT OF CONTINUITY, OR DEVELOPMENT. FIRST SUBJECT. EXAMPLES FROM HAYDN, MOZART, AND BEETHOVEN. CHARACTERISTICS: CLEAR RHYTHM, SIMPLE HARMONY, ADAPTATION FOR WORKING.

I.

I PROPOSE to speak to you about MUSICAL ANALYSIS. You know that, whereas *Synthesis* means *putting together*, *Analysis* means *taking to pieces*. A musical *Composition* is a work in which ideas are placed, or *posed*, in orderly succession and combination. We do not speak of *de*composing a musical work; but we do *analyse*, take it to pieces, find out its several parts, and how they are put together. We shall do this, not in order that you may know how you may put your ideas together, and become composers; but that you may intelligently enjoy the Music that you practise or listen to, by understanding its structure. At the same time, there can be no better training for young composers than the analytical study of the works of the great Masters. A composer may originate beautiful ideas, and we then call him a *Genius*; but he may not have had the training, or may not possess the *mastery* of his resources, requisite to set forth those ideas in the strongest way. Chopin and Dussek— very different composers—were geniuses, but not masters. Hummel was a master, but not a genius. Of course I am expressing my own opinion; but I think it is the general one among mature and competent musicians.

We may as well take a composition of sufficient extent and development, in order to furnish scope and material for analysis. If I were beginning at the other end of the process, I should take short themes, and show you how they can be put together, and welded into a MOVEMENT, which is the term applied to a single complete composition of some considerable length. Instead of this synthetical process, however, we will take a particular *form* of Movement, and analyse it. There are different forms: that is, Movements are constructed on different *plans*. That which I think well to take, in the first instance, is the plan of structure known as SONATA form: more properly *first-movement* form, being that in which the first movement of most *Sonatas, Symphonies,* instrumental *Quartets, Trios,* &c. is usually written. It is also known as the Movement of *Continuity,* or of *Development.* The first term, Continuity, indicates that the Movement has one continuous train of thought, like a narrative or an argument, as distinguished from an *Episodical* Movement, hereafter to be described. The second term, Development, indicates the *unfolding* of ideas, or *Subjects:* the term SUBJECT, in musical terminology, meaning a more or less complete idea, or THEME: this last word signifying a subject *laid down,* as for argument or treatment. The word *Sonata* means *sounded,* or *rung;* just as *Cantata* means *sung.* But a Sonata is now understood to be a composition in at least two, generally three or four, movements, or complete portions (like chapters in a book), for one or more instruments. When for three instruments, the work is usually termed a *Trio:* when for four, a *Quartet:* and so on, the terms *Quintet, Sextet, Septet, Octet, Nonet* being used according to the number of instruments. Such music is termed *chamber,* or *concerted* music. When the composition is *orchestral,*—that is, for a full band of instruments, wind and stringed,—the work is called a SYMPHONY. But the general method of construction, the plan of the movements, is the same in all these cases. There is a difference in the *Concerto,* to be hereafter explained. In old times, however, the term *Concerto* had similar meaning to *Symphony.*

Some of you younger pupils are only advanced enough to practise *Sonatinas;* but a *Sonatina* is simply a *little Sonata,* the plan, in most cases, being the same as that of a larger Sonata. So that you will be able to understand and apply the explanations, all the same.

Briefly, the plan, or order of ideas, in the first movement of a Sonata, or similar work, is this: (*a*) the *first Subject*: then some connecting matter leading to (*b*) the *second Subject*, followed by some supplementary matter, and, probably, a *Codetta*, finishing the *first part* of the movement, at the first *double bar*. Then comes (*c*) the *second part*, or, as some term it, the FREE FANTASIA, which, in the main, consists of the *development* or *working* of the material of the first part. This leads to the *third part* of the movement, which is (*d*) the *Recapitulation*, indicated by the *return of the* (*first*) *Subject*, and the repetition, with modifications, of the matter of the first part; and, sometimes, a *Coda*. This, with some differences and exceptions, is the general outline of the movement that we are considering; and the details I shall describe to you in order.

It will be convenient to consider, in the first instance, movements in the *major mode*, by which we mean beginning and ending in that mode: not at all meaning that there are no *modulations* to the *minor mode*. Some movements that begin in the minor mode terminate in the major, but are spoken of as in the minor. Very rarely do movements begin in the major mode, and end in the minor.

To begin, then, with the *First Subject*, or complete idea, which is in the key of the movement: that which throughout I shall call the *original key*, or TONIC. This *Subject* of a Sonata movement is very different from a *Fugue Subject*, about which I shall speak in another Lecture. This latter consists of a few *single notes*, of marked character, and extends, at the utmost, to a very few bars in length. Whereas, a *Sonata Subject* is of considerable extent: never less than eight bars, and often extending over about a page. Moreover, it is not of single notes, but is *harmonized*, or *accompanied ;* or, in fact, often is so *homogeneous*, consisting so much of interwoven parts, that it could not be represented by single notes.

Here is, firstly, a Subject by Haydn (Sonata No. 30), of eight bars, terminating with a *Perfect Cadence*, or *Full-close :* i. e. the *Dominant* harmony *followed* by that on the *Tonic*. (Ex. 1.)

(1) *Allegro con brio.*

The fourth bar ends with a *Half-close*, or *Imperfect Cadence :* i. e. the *Dominant* harmony *preceded* (in this instance) by the *Tonic*. Thus, this Subject divides itself into two *rhythmical sections*, of equal length, after the manner of verse writing. Music is a *rhythmical language*, with *proportion* in its parts, *parallel* in its phrases, one thing being "set over against another." It has been well said that *Music* gives the "rhythmical arrangement of sounds not articulated, while from the like arrangement of articulate sounds we get the cadences of prose and the measures of verse."* The rhythmical divisions, in Music, are indicated by the more or less decisive, terminal, or restful cadences, in conjunction with the accents. This Subject by Haydn is in *four-bar-rhythm*: an even number of bars to the *Phrase* or *Section*: the two terms being somewhat loosely applied to each division of four bars. This even, regular rhythm is quite the most usual in the first presentation of simple themes, in the older Masters' works at all events. *Irregular* and *broken* rhythms will be considered in another Lecture. They occur, principally, in the development of ideas.

It may be mentioned that the Subject here given is followed by a passage commencing in the same key, which would, by some musicians, be considered a second division of the Subject; but, as this Subject closes so definitely, it seems more natural to regard the passage in question as *intermediate*, leading to the *Second Subject*.

In another Lecture I shall again refer to this same Subject.†
The next Subject is that of Mozart's Sonata, No. 5. (Ex. 2.)

(2) *Allegro.*

* Guest's *History of English Rhythms*, Chap. I. † See Lect. VIII.

This is of ten bars' length. In the Sonata, the last six bars are repeated, with slight variation; this repetition serving, perhaps, to assist in the apprehension of the prolongation of the second Section. For the ten bars are not divided into two Sections of five bars each; but the first Section ends at the fourth (complete) bar, and the second Section, commencing at the third beat of that bar, extends to the end of the Subject. Observe that the two beats of the last (incomplete) bar correspond with the one beat with which the Subject begins.

The next Subject is that of Beethoven's Sonata, op. 10, No. 2. (Ex. 3.) This consists of three Sections of four bars each.

(3) *Allegro.*

I.] FIRST SUBJECT: BEETHOVEN, OP. 10, NO. 2. 9

If the Subject of Mozart's might be considered a *Diptych*,—two-fold,—this may be called a *Triptych*,—three-fold. The first phrase or section, broken into fragments, as by commas, ends with a discord,—the first inversion of the Dominant 7th: it is marked rather by *rhythm* than by *Cadence*. The second phrase briefly touches on the key of the *Sub-dominant*, ending with an *inverted Cadence* in that key. This is not reckoned one of the modulations of the *Movement*, being so brief: only of the *Subject*, which is complete in itself. The third phrase ends with a Perfect Cadence.

Observe how simple these three Subjects are, both in structure and in harmony: little else than *Tonic, Dominant*, and *Sub-dominant* harmonies being used. If I were to give you the following figured basses to fill up, you would think them very easy little exercises, with very little range or variety; and yet they represent the successions of harmonies of the last two Subjects, which are so varied in their forms, or modes of presentation of those harmonies. (Ex. 4, 5.)

One more example from Haydn will illustrate how a little irregularity of rhythm may be balanced and, so to speak, equalized. It is from Sonata No. 28. (Ex. 6.) The Subject con-

(6) *Allegro Moderato.*

sists of eight bars, in three phrases: the first, of three bars, terminating on the first inversion of Tonic harmony; the second, of two bars and a half, terminating with a Perfect Cadence; and the third of the same length, ending in like manner. This Subject, like those previously quoted, contains little but Tonic, Dominant, and Sub-dominant harmonies.

All these Subjects terminate decisively on Tonic harmony. Some Subjects, however, do not end in this manner, but break off with a half-close, or Imperfect Cadence: that is, on Dominant harmony. This is somewhat as though a novelist gave only a partial delineation of his hero, before introducing the heroine, and bringing about incidents. Such is the case in Beethoven's Sonata, Op. 49, No. 2, in G major, where the half-close, bars 14 and 15, simply introduces the prolonged dominant bass, which terminates at bar 20; and then comes the second Subject. The same absence of a full close of the Subject is to be observed in Mozart's Symphony in C, known as the "*Jupiter*" (first movement).

Again, some Subjects are of considerable length, and consist of several *Sections*, properly so called, or *portions*, divisible into *Phrases*. A notable example is that of Beethoven's Sonata, Op. 28, known as the "*Pastoral*" (though not so called by the composer). This Subject extends to twenty-nine bars; and consists of a Section of ten bars, reiterated: then another Section of eight bars, reiterated, with a codetta (little tail-piece) formed from the previous phrase. Similarly, the same master's Sonata, Op. 31, No. 3; the first Subject of which may be considered as terminating at bar 29, and is broken into phrases, which are easily discernible.

Besides these matters of rhythmical division, there are other features in good Subjects, such as those which we have been examining, which will better be considered when we are studying the *development* of Movements; as these features have to do with the *suggestiveness* of the Subjects: the *workable material* in them. I can hardly help the anomaly of using the word *material* to designate that which is purely *mental*. One feature you may easily notice : the number of small *figures, fragments, motivi,* as they are termed, which may be, so to speak, detached from the Subject, for separate treatment.

LECTURE II.

FIRST MOVEMENTS IN THE MAJOR MODE, *continued*. SECOND SUBJECT, AND CONNECTING PASSAGES.

II.

HAVING considered the *first Subject* of a Sonata movement in a Major key, we have now to proceed to the *second Subject*. This is, in most cases, in the *Dominant,*—the 5th of the original key. There are notable exceptions which I shall tell you about in the next Lecture. This second Subject in a new key is not taken at once, however, on the conclusion of the first Subject, except in some very concise Movements, or Sonatinas; but is approached by means of *Modulation*. If the new key were taken promptly, without any *modulating process*, we should call that *plunge* into, or start in, the new key, a *Transition*, rather than a Modulation. But that is not the usual method of proceeding in this kind of Movement, being less of the nature of *continuity*, which is one of its characteristic features.

I may here say that in some of the earlier compositions of the class that we are considering, the general outline is observable in the order of keys,—*Tonic* and *Dominant*, for the first part, related keys for the second part, return to the Subject and key;—but often *without any clearly defined second Subject*, of a contrasted character. The portion in the new key is rather a *continuation*, or second part of the first Subject. This you will find to be the case in many of the *Suites* and *Partitas* of Bach, Handel, and other writers of early period; these compositions having been the precursors of the *Sonata* as we now have it. The *germ* of the more fully developed plan is therein visible. Take, for instance, the *Allegro* of Handel's second *Suite*. (Ex. 7.) The first four

(7) *Allegro.*

bars, truly, may be said to be complete in themselves, terminating with a *full-close;* but that which immediately follows, albeit that it is in the *Dominant,*—C major,—is so uncontrasted, so similar in movement, as hardly to be termed a second *Subject:* it is more like a carrying on of the original thought, but with the excursion to the related key. You will find similar instances in the *Allemandes* of Bach's *Suites Françaises,* Nos. 5 and 6. We shall also notice the same

II.] APPROACHING THE SECOND SUBJECT. BEETHOVEN. 17

thing when we examine Movements of short dimensions in subsequent Lectures.

In some Movements, instead of a modulating process of progression to the key of the Dominant, the *first Subject* does not end with a *full-close*, but comes to a *half-close*, as we saw in the last Lecture; and this being *on* the Dominant *harmony*,—not *in* the Dominant *key*,—the Dominant harmony is at once *assumed*, so to speak, as a *new Tonic*, and the *second Subject* forthwith commences in that new key, so reached. This is the case in Beethoven's Sonata in G major, Op. 49, No. 2, referred to in the last Lecture. (Ex. 8.)

Although, in bars 14, 15, there occurs what might be considered a modification of a close *in* D major, yet, the fact that the Dominant chord to that key is only in an inverted form,—which is not powerful,—and then the recurrence, in the continued passage *on* D, of the Dominant 7th in the original key, combine to give the impression of the close at bar 20 being *imperfect:* then follows the second Subject, in D.

A similar example occurs in Mozart's Sonata, No. 16, commencing thus:—(Ex. 9.) Bars 10 to 12 (Ex. 10) give, in like manner to the example from Beethoven, a *half-close*.

Then, however, most dexterously, bar 13 implies the Dominant to the new key, and the *second Subject enters at bar* 14.

In other Movements, a half-close on the *Dominant of the new key* is made, prior to the entry of the *second Subject*. This may imply some anticipation of the change of key, and needs much adeptness to avoid the impression of a *double-dominant*. (See my *Text-book of Music*, § 345.) In Mozart's Sonata, No. 7 (Ex. 11), the modulating passage terminates

(11) *Allegro con spirito.*

with a *half-close* on D; and then the two bars of—so to speak—*poising* on the Dominant harmony introduce the *second Subject*. (Ex. 12.)

But now we must look at this modulating process. The

(12)

2nd Subject.

methods of modulation, so far as the harmonies are concerned, many of you understand, more or less. But then, as I say to you in class sometimes, skill is required to effect the modulation in such a way as to introduce the new key,—I had almost said, unawares: at all events, without parade, or formality: naturally, and, moreover, in keeping with the flow of the music: sometimes so as to lead to the *second Subject*, in the new key, as a felt *result*, or *climax*, or *restful* point. In many cases, instead of such half-closes or dividing-lines as those that I have quoted, the *second Subject* is linked on with such insinuating charm that all seems continuous. Some figure or *motivo*, drawn from the *first Subject*, is frequently made use of for modulating working.

I can only call your attention to a few instances to illustrate that which I have just stated.

In Beethoven's Sonata, Op. 14, No. 1, the first phrase of the *Subject* is Ex. 13. The modulating passage commences

simultaneously with the termination of the *Subject*, at bar 13 (Ex. 14), and consists of an extension of the opening of

BEETHOVEN, OP. 14, NO. 1.

the *Subject*, and a reiteration of the little semiquaver figure of bar 4, the Pedal-bass character being kept up, and the unity thus preserved. The third and fourth bars, moreover, of this passage, are formed by an *augmentation*—*i. e.* taking in longer notes—of the left-hand passage of bars 9 and 10 of the *Subject*. (Ex. 15.)

Another instructive example is from Beethoven's Sonata, Op. 31 (or 29), No. 3; which, moreover, presents points for comment, upon which I had better dwell at once, even though I digress from the matter which we are specially considering.

The *Subject* opens with these eight bars (Ex. 16), which are repeated with change of register. The first harmony, which has been known as the *added* 6th (Rameau's theory),

BEETHOVEN, OP. 31, NO. 3.

you know, from our class-lessons, is now considered the third inversion of the chord of the 11th, root B♭; and proceeds (bar 4) to diminished 7th on A, root F, *Supertonic* of the key. This proceeds (bar 6) to second inversion of Tonic harmony, which is followed by a *full-close.* We shall recur to this *Subject* in another Lecture, for further instruction. After the reiteration, some fragmentary passages (Ex. 17) lead to Ex. 18. Observe how easily the modulation is

introduced; but even this new *Tonic*, B♭, is for a while treated rather as though it were a *Dominant*. At bar 7 of this extract the *Subject* is again referred to, with the *Minor* (instead of *Major*) 9th, C♭, to the root; and by a few bars drawn from the second figure of the *Subject*, the chord of the *Augmented* 6th on G♭ is reached, and then, by the Dominant harmony, the *second Subject*. Bars 17, 18 give by augment-

ation the figure of bar 3 of Ex. 17. Thus, from the beginning to the *second Subject*, all *hangs together;* and, pedal-bass apart, the whole *first Subject* is built on the simple harmonies indicated in Ex. 19. This, with similar examples in our

last Lecture (pp. 8, 9), may show some of you what *may* be done to impart interest to apparently unpromising, or, at least, very limited, figured basses, such as you have to work.

Another beautiful example is furnished in the Sonata of Beethoven, Op. 10, No. 2, of which the *Subject* was given in the last Lecture (p. 8). After that *Subject* the following few bars occur (Ex. 20), which are obviously suggested by

the *Subject*. The effect on the ear of the chord of the *Augmented* 6th, in its so-called *German* form (see my *Text-book*, § 349), is that of a 7th—E♭—on F; but the *enharmonic* change is made which leads to a *half-close* in A minor, and this diversion renders the entry of the *second Subject* charmingly welcome. The enharmonic is sufficiently dwelt upon to prevent undue abruptness: a point sometimes neglected by young writers. A similar instance of a *half-*

close on E, to precede the *second Subject* in C, occurs in Mr. Prout's admirably constructed Symphony in F, No. 3.

In Beethoven's Sonata, Op. 22, the *Subject* of which commences thus (Ex. 21), and ends with a close on the *Tonic*,

bar 8, the following passage (Ex. 22), on the figure of the *Subject*, leads to a *half-close*, succeeded by yet another passage drawn from the *Subject*, bars 11, 12, and then a modulating passage, bars 13 to 15, leading to a half-close in F, bar 16,

the passage on the *Dominant* of that key terminating thus (Ex. 23), the connecting scale-passage linking on the *second Subject* by being responded to in the left-hand.

In early writers, Haydn and Mozart, the *second Subject* was not unfrequently of very similar character to the *first;* in fact, almost a variation of it, in the new key, at least in its earlier phrases. Thus, in Haydn's Sonata, No. 5, the first phrase

of the *first Subject* consists of these six bars (Ex. 24), and the *second Subject* commences thus (Ex. 25). The similarity

(25)

is obvious. The first four bars of his Sonata No. 29 are (Ex. 26): the *second Subject* commences thus (Ex. 27).

(26) *Allegro moderato.*

SECOND SUBJECT SOMETIMES LIKE THE FIRST.

Observe the *imitation* between the second half of bar 4, and the first half of bar 5: small indeed, but one of those small things which are characteristic of *unity* of thought.

His Sonata No. 32, again, has its *first Subject* commencing thus (Ex. 28), the *second Subject* thus (Ex. 29). In these cases, however, some entirely new material succeeds the commencements here given; just illustrating how, in Music as in other matters, an initial idea may give rise to different trains of thought.

32 LECTURES ON MUSICAL ANALYSIS. [LECT.

II.]   SECOND SUBJECT LIKE THE FIRST.   33

(29)

In Mozart's Sonata No. 2, the *first Subject* begins thus (Ex. 30). Observe the bass, bars 1 and 2. The *second*

Subject commences with the *arpeggio figure* in the bass, taken by *inverse movement*, after the *triplet* passage. (Ex. 31, bar 5.) This triplet passage, moreover, recurs, slightly

11.] COMBINED FIGURES. 35

altered, in the second portion of this *second Subject*: compare bars 5 and 16.

The *first Subject* of Mozart's Sonata No. 18 (of which there is also a version with violin accompaniment) begins

D 2

thus (Ex. 32). The two figures of this are brought together for the *second Subject*. (Ex. 33.)

A similar example to those here cited of likeness between first and second Subjects is referred to in my *Text-book*, page 212, Figs. 353, 354.

Much more usual, however, is it for the *second Subject* to be quite different, in character and in rhythmical figure, from the *first Subject*, as in the Examples from Beethoven already given. If the *first Subject* be of a somewhat *bravura* (brave, spirited) or *risoluto* (resolute) character, the *second Subject* is frequently of a more tender *cantabile* (singing) character: the two being somewhat in the relation of hero and heroine in a novel. And, as in such analogical case, there will be forethought about their availableness for mutual working in the development of the movement, as we shall hereafter see (Lecture VII). Whereas a *Fugue* may be considered as a *monograph*,—*one* theme being dwelt upon, and more or less exhaustively worked out; in a *Sonata movement*, such as we are considering, on the other hand, we are interested in the connected workings of at least two principal themes, with some of a subordinate kind, as in the characters of a novel or drama. We are mainly interested in *Romeo* and *Juliet*, but we cannot dispense with *Friar Laurence*, or the garrulous *Nurse*.

LECTURE III.

MOVEMENTS IN THE MAJOR MODE, *continued*. SECOND SUBJECT IN OTHER KEYS THAN THE DOMINANT. INSTANCES OF FALSE NOTATION, AND IMPLIED ENHARMONICS. MOVEMENTS IN THE MINOR MODE.

III.

You will quite understand the fitness of that which I have told you, and which you must have observed for yourselves, that the *second Subject* of Movements in the *Major Mode* is generally in the key of the *Dominant*, that being the most natural key to which to modulate, on account of the Tetrachord in common between the two keys. (See *Text-book*, §§ 53, 352.) So natural, indeed, is it to modulate to that key, that some weak composers even make a modulation in the *second Subject* itself, to the Dominant of the key in which that is written, which is a weakness, besides being too remote from the original key of the Movement, before the memory of that key has passed away. It is worth your while to observe how this weakness is avoided by the great masters, Haydn, Mozart, and Beethoven, especially in the kind of Movement that we are considering.

But there are some instances to be noticed in which the *second Subject* of *Major* Movements is *not* in the key of the *Dominant*, but in some other key having affinity with the original key.

In Beethoven's Sonata in A major, Op. 2, No. 2, commencing (Ex. 34), the *second Subject* begins in E *minor*, which is not the *true Dominant* to A, not having the *Leading note* to that key. (Ex. 35.) By a somewhat unusual progression through G, B flat, &c.,—very transient, however,—the harmony of the Dominant minor 9th is reached, and I need not tell

(34) *Allegro vivace.*

you that this may be resolved either to the *Major* or to the *Minor* chord on the *Tonic*. Beethoven resolves it on the *Major* harmony, and in that key the first part closes.

(35)   2nd Subject.

III.]   IMPLIED ENHARMONICS.   43

Observe the *implied*, not *expressed* enharmonic change in bars 3 and 4 of this Subject. The root of bar 3 is B, dominant of E, the E (with ornamental F) being an *Appoggiatura* to D♯, which latter note is really changed to E♭ in bar 4, though not so written, with the root D♮, dominant to G. Similarly, the F♯ in bar 7 is the major 3rd in the chord of the minor 9th on D, dominant to G, and is in bar 8, by implication, changed enharmonically to G♭, minor 9th of F♮, dominant to B♭.

I digress in this way to call your attention to any noteworthy point for you, as students of harmony, to observe in any Subject or passage that comes before us; and I do not think that you will be diverted by such a digression from the main line of thought, which, just now, is the exceptional keys for the *second Subject*.

In Beethoven's Sonata in C major, Op. 2, No. 3, the modulating passage after the termination of the *first Subject* has a half-close on G, the passage itself having the harmony of G major prominent. But the *second Subject* then begins in G minor (Ex. 36), the change of mode not being abrupt

(36) *Allegro con brio.*

III.] DIVISIONS OF SECOND SUBJECT. 45

after the single note close, with the subsequent rests. This *second Subject*, first portion, is noticeable, firstly, for its rhythm, a phrase of two bars succeeded by one of four bars, and this rhythmical structure repeated. Secondly, its discursiveness, through C minor, D minor, and A minor, in which key it makes a close, though not in decisive manner. This is followed by a *risoluto* passage leading to a close on the Dominant harmony of G, on which harmony a brief passage leads to a tranquil, singing theme in G major. (Ex. 37.) This may be regarded as the *second division* of the *second Subject*. But at this point of my explanation it may be well, once for all, to say that musicians differ in their way

of analyzing such a succession of themes. According to some, all that portion which is in the same key, or even has the same *Tonic*, with difference of *mode*, is to be considered as constituting *one Subject*, though in two or more portions, or divisions. According to others, each fresh portion, with a clearly defined commencement, such as the theme that is now before us, is a *new Subject*. So that these analyzers would consider this as a *third Subject*, or else as the *second Subject proper*, regarding all that portion from the beginning in G minor to this G major theme as *intermediate*, or as preamble. The adoption of one or the other methods of classification will depend upon the more or less manifest connection between the several portions or themes. Similar instances will come before us in other works.

This theme is worthy of your special notice for its beautiful imitational structure: the middle part answering the upper in the first instance, and this order being afterwards reversed. The expected close in G is averted by a *bravura* passage of eight bars, followed by a syncopated passage, with a series of suspensions in the bass, leading to a close, and then a *Codetta*.

III.] EXCEPTIONAL KEYS FOR SECOND SUBJECT. 47

But this Sonata movement only so far deviates from the usual plan in the *commencement* of the *second Subject*, as we have considered it, being in G *minor*, not the true *Dominant* to the original key, on account of the absence of the *Leading note* to that key. The true *Dominant* is afterwards reached, however, and in that key the *first part* of the Movement finishes. For similar instances see Beethoven's Sonatas for Pianoforte and Violin, Op. 12, No. 2, and Op. 30, No. 3.

There are other instances, however, in which the departure from the usual plan is much more decided. In three of Beethoven's Sonatas in the Major Mode, the *second Subject* is in the key of the *Mediant*.

In the Sonata Op. 31, No. 1, the *first Subject* of which commences (Ex. 38), and is itself remarkable for its discur-

siveness of key, passing rapidly from G through D, F, and C, the *second Subject* commences in B major (Ex. 39), and then passes to B minor, with the theme itself as the bass, and in that key the *first part* finishes. Except in the most

48   LECTURES ON MUSICAL ANALYSIS.   [LECT.

transient way, there is no modulation to the *Dominant* throughout the Movement.

Similarly, in the Sonata Op. 53, the *first Subject* of which commences (Ex. 40), the *second Subject* (Ex. 41) is in E

SECOND SUBJECT IN THE MEDIANT.

major, at the close of which a *Codetta* is added in E minor, in which key the first part terminates,—a short modulating passage leading back to C major, the original key, for the repeat. There is no modulation to the *Dominant* in this Movement.

(41)

The same is the case in the Sonata in B flat, Op. 106, the *second Subject* of which is in G major, commencing (Ex. 42), and there is no modulation to the *Dominant*.

(42) *Allegro.*

A similar instance occurs in Beethoven's Overture to *Leonora*, Op. 72, known as No. 3 (as well as in the other version, having the same *Opus* number, but known as No. 2), the key of which work is C major, the *second Subject* (of the *Allegro*) being in E major. (Ex. 43.) A very remark-

able change of key must be noticed in this Subject, effected (like those above referred to in the Sonata Op. 2, No. 2) by an enharmonic, implied, not expressed. The B♭ in bar 7 would be A♯ in relation to the harmony immediately preceding it, with F♯ as root. The C♯, on the other hand, would be D♭ in relation to that which succeeds it, the root being then C♮, dominant to F, to which key it so beautifully proceeds, returning by a sequential progression to E major, in which key the *first part* closes.

III.] SECOND SUBJECT IN THE SUB-MEDIANT. 51

In Beethoven's Trio in B♭ for Pianoforte, Violin, and Violoncello, Op. 97, the *first Subject* of which commences

(Ex. 44), the *second Subject* is in the key of the *Sub-mediant*, G major, commencing thus (Ex. 45):—

Another instance may be referred to, that of Beethoven's Quintet for stringed instruments, Op. 29, in C major, commencing (Ex. 46). After this section has been repeated in

E 2

varied guise, a triplet passage, of which Ex. 47 gives the last two bars and a half, has an *interrupted cadence*, leading

BEETHOVEN'S QUINTET, OP. 29.

abruptly to the key of A minor, in which key there is an imitational passage founded on the *first Subject*, which ultimately leads to a *half-close*, shortly followed by the *second Subject*, commencing in A major (Ex. 48), but soon

returning to A minor, in which key the *first part* closes. The key of the *Dominant*, G major, has only transient reference throughout the Movement.

It is now time to speak of Movements in the *Minor* key, that is, with the *first Subject* in that Mode.

With regard to the *first Subject* of such Movements, there is nothing special to say beyond that which I have already said in speaking of *Major* Movements. Except, indeed, one point to which I would call your attention: namely, the purity of tonality observable in the Subjects in the Minor Mode by the great masters; the single-minded adherence to the *Tonic*, without coquetting with the so-called *relative major*, vacillating between two Tonics. However the *minor seventh* of the scale may be introduced *melodically*, it is not used as a *harmony* note, unless for an avowed modulation, or for special chromatic effects. To impress this thought upon you, this *fact*, I may rather say, I cite some complete Subjects.

That of Haydn's Sonata No. 13, in B minor, is almost entirely built on Tonic and Dominant harmonies. And then how welcome in its simplicity is the A♮, ushering in the new key, in which, after a *half-close*, the *second Subject* enters. (Ex. 49.)

HAYDN'S SONATA IN B MINOR.

This key, the *major* key of the *Mediant*, or, as it is commonly styled, the *relative major* to the original key, is that in which the *second Subject* of Minor Movements is usually written, though by no means invariably, as I shall show you.

Another beautiful subject, that of Haydn's Sonata No. 23, in G minor, illustrates the same point. It is free from any suggestion of B♭ major, being entirely composed of the simplest harmonies of its own key. Observe the beautiful effect, so simple, of the added upper part in bar 3. (Ex. 50.) Then, in bar 6, by the most natural introduction of the

III.] SUBJECTS IN MINOR MODE. 57

Dominant 7th in B♭, that key is reached, and, after a half-close, the *second Subject* enters. (Ex. 51.)

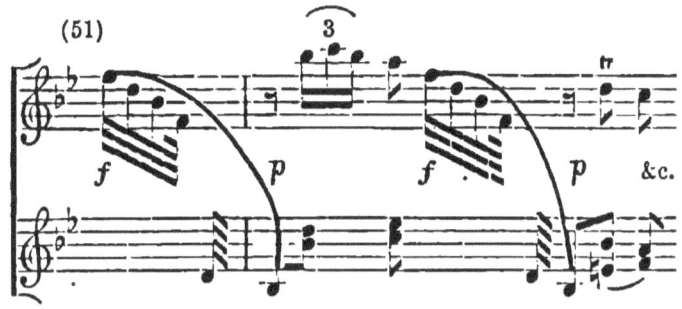

The same feature is observable in Haydn's Sonata No. 27, in C minor; and in No. 31, in C♯ minor. (Ex. 52.) This latter, moreover, affords another example of that which I told you in the last lecture about the *second Subject*, in some Movements by the older masters, being partly founded

58 LECTURES ON MUSICAL ANALYSIS. [LECT.

2nd Subject.

on the first. The Sonata before us has a short Subject entirely in the primary key, closing at bar 6; then a modulating passage, ending on the first inversion of the *Dominant* 7th in E, followed by the *second Subject* in that key. The first portion of this presents the first figure of the *first Subject* in a new guise, and the second portion is derived from the second and succeeding bars of that *Subject*.

Mozart's two Sonatas in the Minor Mode have the same structure, in that the *first Subject*, in both cases, is entirely in the original key; and the *second Subject* is in the *major* key of the *Mediant*. No. 8, in A minor, after the *first Subject*, commencing, Ex. 53, has a modulating passage

(53) *Allegro maestoso.*

in which C minor is prominent; and the *second Subject*, in C major, commencing, Ex. 54, comes with freshness. I shall have to recur to this Sonata more than once.

No. 14 has a *first Subject* of eighteen bars, commencing, Ex. 55, entirely in C minor, followed by a modulating

passage of four bars, derived from that Subject, leading to the *second Subject* in E♭, which is of considerable extent, if all in that key is to be considered as one Subject, having, it may be said, three principal divisions as follows (Examples 56, 57, 58), and then the Codetta.

Beethoven's Sonata in F minor, Op. 2, No. 1, is of very

III.] MOVEMENTS IN THE MINOR MODE. 61

(56)

(57)

(58)

clear construction. There is no *full-close* to the *first Subject* (Ex. 59); but after the half-close at bar 8, a modulating passage, built on the *first Subject*, leads to the *second Subject*, in A♭, which, you will observe, begins with the *minor* 9th

(59) *Allegro.*

on the *Dominant*. This, as you know from your lessons, frequently occurs in the *major* key, being, by some theorists, termed *Chromatic* when so occurring. (Ex. 60.)

Beethoven's Sonata in C minor, Op. 10, No. 1, has a Subject extending over thirty bars, beginning (Ex. 61), and ending (Ex. 62) entirely in the key. After a silent bar, a transitional passage, almost as defined as a new Subject, passes through A♭, F minor, and D♭, to a passage on a B♭ *pedal bass*, ushering in the *second Subject* in E♭ major. (Ex. 63.)

III.] BEETHOVEN'S OP. 10, NO. 1. 63

The lovely Sonatina in G minor, Op. 49, No. 1 (Ex. 64), after the *half-close* at bar 8, proceeds to diverge to B♭ major, in which key the *second Subject* enters, bar 16, extending over fourteen bars; when a *Codetta* of four bars, founded on the *second Subject*, concludes the first part.

(64) *Andante.*

III.] BEETHOVEN'S OP. 57: FIRST SUBJECT. 65

The Sonata in F minor, Op. 57, commonly called "*appassionata*" (not so termed by Beethoven), though of such

(65) *Allegro assai.*

F

extended proportions, does not, in its Subject, touch on the key of A♭ (Ex. 65). It seems momentarily to touch on the key of D♭, in bars 7 and 8. The entry of the *Subject* on the harmony of G♭ is considered as a Chromatic progression, not a modulation, there being no modulating chords. The chord marked * in bar 7 is an instance of false notation,—perhaps for simplicity's sake. As it stands, the root is F, on which G♭ is the minor 9th, and A♮ the major 3rd. But the resolution to the harmony of D♭ shows that A♭ is the root of the chord, and that the A♮ should be B♭♭, the minor 9th to the root.

The *second Subject* may be considered, as above explained,

BEETHOVEN'S OP. 57: SECOND SUBJECT.

to consist of two divisions: the first, approached and commenced (Ex. 66). The E♭ in bar 1 of the extract is an *inverted dominant pedal note* in the key of A♭. In bar 3 occurs another instance of false notation; the E♮ should be F♭, minor 9th to the dominant. The *second division* of the *second Subject* commences (Ex. 67) in A♭ minor, in which key the first part of the Movement terminates.

LECTURE IV.

MOVEMENTS IN MINOR MODE, *continued.* MISTAKEN NOTION ABOUT THIS MODE. SECOND SUBJECT NOT ALWAYS IN MAJOR KEY OF THE MEDIANT. SOMETIMES IN MINOR KEY OF THE DOMINANT: IN MAJOR KEY OF SUB-MEDIANT. THE RECAPITULATION: RETURN TO ORIGINAL KEY AND FIRST SUBJECT. EXCEPTIONAL CASES FROM MOZART AND BEETHOVEN. METHODS OF RETURNING. SECOND SUBJECT IN VARIOUS KEYS IN THE RECAPITULATION. EXAMPLES FROM MOZART, MENDELSSOHN; BENNETT, ETC. WITH ALL VARIETIES, ESSENTIAL FEATURES PRESERVED.

IV.

IN the Movements in the Minor Mode which we have already considered, the *second Subject* has been in the Major key of the *Mediant* or Minor 3rd of the key, generally termed the *Relative Major*, as distinguished from the *Tonic Major*. This makes a contrast, by a certain brightness, to the Minor Mode of the *first Subject*. Do not, however, fall into the popular error of associating the idea of melancholy with the Minor Mode, as though the two words were almost synonyms. There is a certain sentiment about the Minor Mode which is hardly to be defined in words, any more than other things about music, but it is not necessarily melancholy. No one would think of applying this term, for instance, to the song, "*O ruddier than the cherry*," in Handel's *Acis and Galatea;* but that is in the key of G minor. On the other hand, how solemn in its expression of grief is the Dead March in "*Saul*," which is in C major, with only one brief modulation to the Minor Mode. Still, there is, undoubtedly, a brightness of effect in having the *second Subject* in the Major Mode, after the *first Subject* has been in the Minor.

A partial exception to this more usual order occurred in Beethoven's Sonata Op. 57, in which, as I showed you, a considerable portion in A♭ minor followed that in A♭ major. (See Ex. 66, 67.)

An exception of the reverse kind occurs in Beethoven's Sonata in C minor, Op. 13 (the *pathetic*), in which the

72   LECTURES ON MUSICAL ANALYSIS.   [LECT.

second Subject of the first Movement may be divided into three portions: the *first* commencing (Ex. 68) in E♭ minor, the *second* (Ex. 69) and *third* (Ex. 70) being in E♭ major.

But there is another procedure in many Movements in the Minor Mode : that of having the *second Subject* in the *Minor* key of the *Dominant* of the original scale, not that generally spoken of as the *Dominant key*, there being no *leading note* to the original key in this *Minor* key.

This is the plan of Beethoven's Sonata in D minor, Op. 31, No. 2, commencing (Ex. 71).

Let us linger a little, however, to consider this *first Subject*, which is exceptional. The *Largo* on the first inversion of the *Dominant* chord might appear, to a superficial observer, to be a mere *start*, like the first chord of a *Recitative*. But it is much more than this, it does more than usher in the agitated *Allegro* figure. It reappears at bar 7 on another harmony, that of C major; and, having thus *alternated* with that agitated portion, reappears in *Allegro* time, as the bass of the more regular theme, commencing at bar 21 (Ex. 72),

and is reiterated, in similar form, bars 25, 29, &c. It is made much of in the *second part*, or *development* of the Movement.

The passage commencing at bar 41 (Ex. 73), after the

half-close on the *Dominant* chord in A minor, being a carrying on of the agitated figure already referred to, may be considered as a *poising* on that bass, notwithstanding the alternating harmony of A minor, rather than as the *second Subject*, which is reached subsequently. (Ex. 74.) The first

IV.] SECOND SUBJECT IN MINOR KEY OF DOMINANT. 75

part ends in this key of A minor. The key of F major is not even transiently touched on throughout the Movement.

The same structure is to be observed in the *last* Movement of this Sonata, which also is a Movement of continuity.

It is stated by one of Beethoven's biographers that, being asked for the clue to this Sonata and the Op. 57, their "*poetic basis*," as it would now-a-days be termed, he replied, "*Read Shakspeare's 'Tempest.'*"

The *last* Movement of the Sonata in C♯ minor, Op. 27, No. 2, absurdly called the "Moonlight," is also of the same structure, the *second Subject*, in both its divisions (Ex. 75, 76), or as others may very well and reasonably term them,

the *second* and *third Subjects*, being in G♯ minor, in which key the first part ends. No portion, either of the *first Subject* or of the rest of the Movement, touches on the key of E major.

So it is with the first Movement of Beethoven's Sonata in E minor, Op. 90. The key of G major is, indeed, transiently touched in the *first Subject*, but not elsewhere in the Movement; the *second Subject*, and the remaining portion of the *first part*, being in B minor.

This is the order of keys also in Mendelssohn's Symphony in A minor, termed the *Scotch*. The *first Subject* of the *Allegro* commences (Ex. 77); and the second Subject (Ex. 78),

beautifully superposed on the figure of that *first Subject*, is in E minor, and in that key the *first part* closes.

There are similar examples in the *last Movement* of Beethoven's Sonatas Op. 2, No. 1, and Op. 57, in the first

IV.]   BEETHOVEN'S UNCONVENTIONALISM.   HIS OP. 111.   77

Movement of his Sonata for pianoforte and violin, in A minor, Op. 23, &c.

I cannot recall any instances of this structure in the works of Haydn or Mozart, nor, indeed, in those of any composer prior to Beethoven, who seems to have originated this departure from the conventional practice; but not, observe, from orderly structure and arrangement of Subjects. Do not think, moreover, that departure from conventionality was the distinguishing proof or manifestation of his genius. He adhered to accepted order much more than he departed from it.

In Beethoven's Sonata in C minor, Op. 111, the first modulation in the *Allegro* is to A♭ major, in which key there is a short theme. (Ex. 79.) Though this is not the so-called *Relative Major*, but the major key of the *Sub-mediant*,

the contrast of modes is still preserved. And in the instances above mentioned, in which both Subjects are in the Minor Mode, it is for the preservation of a particular sentiment. In none of these cases is there any wanton defiance of orderly principles.

The slow Movement of Beethoven's Sonata in B♭, Op. 106, is in F♯ minor, commencing (Ex. 80). The *second*

(80) *Adagio sostenuto.*

una corda   *mezza voce*   &c.

Subject, like that of the Movement just referred to, is in the key of the Sub-mediant, D major. (Ex. 81.)

(81)

&c.

In order to complete the consideration of the *second Subject*, especially in Movements in the Minor Mode, I must now anticipate, and tell you about the RECAPITULATION, which, you will remember, I described as the *third part* of a *Movement of continuity*. I am aware that the *second part* has not yet been considered; but that will be the subject of subsequent Lectures.

THE RECAPITULATION OR THIRD PART.

This *third part* of the Movement consists generally of the *Recapitulation* or *retrospect* of the matter of the *first part*, with such alteration or modification as is requisite to bring the Movement to a termination in the *original key*, instead of in the *Dominant*, or such other key as the *first part* finished in. In addition to this, a *Coda* is sometimes appended. Moreover, there are sometimes varieties in the mode of presentation, not resulting from the avoidance of modulation, but prompted by the fancy or scholarship of the composer.

Almost invariably, the return to the *original key* is simultaneous with the re-entry of the *first Subject*, with or without modification or embellishment. It is so in all the Sonata Movements of Haydn, Mozart, and Beethoven hitherto quoted, with two exceptions, these being No. 16 of Mozart's, and Beethoven's Op. 10, No. 2. In that by Mozart (see Ex. 9, p. 18), the return to the *first Subject* is in the key of F, from which C major as a *Dominant* is reached, and the same half-close as Ex. 10 precedes the *second Subject* in C instead of in G. In that by Beethoven (see Ex. 3, p. 8), the whole ten bars of the *Subject* reappear in D major, from which a modulation is made, with beautiful simplicity, to the original key (Ex. 82), in which the last eight bars of the Subject are then repeated, followed immediately by the *second Subject* in F; the few bars (see Ex. 20) which originally interposed between the two Subjects being

(82) end of Subject.

omitted, the modulating bars just quoted having been of the same kind.

These are exceptional cases, however; the reappearance of the *first Subject* is almost always in the original key, though not unfrequently in altered guise. And frequently the method of return, after the *working*, is an opportunity for consummate skill to render the reappearance of the Subject a surprise, or a point of grateful repose, and to link it in continuity with the working. For this latter feature observe, as an instance, the sequence of Suspensions (in the bass), with the triplet figure from the *first Subject* (see Ex. 59, p. 61), with which the return is introduced in Beethoven's Sonata Op. 2, No. 1. (Ex. 83.)

IV.] MODIFICATIONS IN THE RECAPITULATION. 81

Very insinuating is the return in the Sonata by Beethoven Op. 31, No. 3 (see Ex. 16, p. 22), on the harmony of F minor, to which there had been a modulation, without any indication, by Dominant harmony or otherwise, of the approach to the original key. (Ex. 84.)

This very prominent incident in a Movement—the return to the original key and Subject—will be better considered, however, in connection with the *second part*, the end of which is marked by this return.

But that which invites our attention now is the *modification* of the *first Subject*, or of the connecting matter, or of both, in the *Recapitulation*, in order to the avoidance of the modulation which was effected in the *first part*, and the proper re-introduction of the *second Subject* in the *Tonic* (generally), instead of in the *Dominant* or other relative key. It is for this purpose that I anticipate the *Recapitulation* in this Lecture, so that we may complete our consideration of the *second Subject*. I can give only a few illustrations of the methods in which this may be effected.

In Haydn's Sonata No. 28, after the Subject has been recapitulated without alteration of Ex. 6, instead of the original modulating passage, through F minor to the Dominant harmony of E♭ (Ex. 85), the Subject is reiterated, with modification, in A♭ minor, so leading to the Dominant harmony of that original Tonic (Ex. 86), and subsequently the *second Subject* in the *Tonic Major* comes with freshness.

G

(85) *Allegro moderato.*

(86)

&c.

In Haydn's Sonata No. 23, a prolongation of the second phrase of the *first Subject* (bar 3 of Ex. 50, p. 56), instead of a close in the key, introduces the *second Subject* in G minor, instead of in B♭ major, thus presenting it in new guise. (Ex. 87.) This same presentation of the *second Subject* in different Mode, Minor for Major, occurs in his Sonata in B minor, No. 13, quoted in Ex. 49.

In Mozart's Sonata No. 8, in A minor, after the recurrence in the *Recapitulation* of the eight bars of the *first Subject* (see Ex. 53), instead of the fresh start of that Subject,

(87)

followed by a diversion to C major (Ex. 88), there is introduced a passage founded on that *first Subject*, taken this time in the bass, and prolonged, with slight divergence,

(88) *Allegro maestoso.*

in the original key of A minor (Ex. 89), in which, subsequently, the *second Subject* occurs; another instance of the change of Mode in the presentation of a Subject.

(89)

&c.

In Mozart's Sonata No. 14, in C minor (see Ex. 55), instead of the concise modulation to E♭ (Ex. 90), the

(90) *Allegro molto.*

&c.

passage is thus diverted by imitational working, and a singing passage, not previously appearing in the Movement (Ex. 91), is substituted for that in Ex. 56, followed by that

(91)

which was in E♭ major (see Ex. 57), now in C minor, from which there is no departure through the remainder of the Movement.

In Beethoven's Sonata Op. 14, No. 1 (see Ex. 13), in the *Recapitulation*, after the passage in Ex. 15, reiterated, instead of the modulating passage, Ex. 14, an *interrupted cadence* of surprising effect gives a modification of the Subject in the key of C, from which, by the chord of the *Augmented* 6th, the Dominant of E is reached, followed by the *second Subject* in that key. This is a beautiful instance, but quite inimitable—it is a stroke of genius.

In his Sonata Op. 31, No. 3 (see Ex. 16), the passage at Ex. 18 is, in the *Recapitulation*, curtailed by the omission of the allusion to the *first Subject;* the previous Dominant harmony, slightly extended, leading to the *second Subject* in the original Tonic.

In those cases, however, in which the *second Subject* appears originally in some other key than the *Dominant*, it sometimes appears in the *Recapitulation* in some other key than the *Tonic*. Thus in Beethoven's Sonata Op. 31, No. 1 (see Examples 38, 39), the *second Subject*, which in the first part is in the key of the *Mediant*, B major and minor, is introduced in the *Recapitulation* in the *Submediant*, E major and minor, after which latter key the resumption of the original Tonic, G, is easily effected.

Precisely the same order of keys holds good in the Sonata Op. 53 (see Examples 40, 41), the *second Subject* being in the *Mediant* in the first instance, and entering in the *Submediant*, A major, in the *Recapitulation*, for the first four bars, soon passing back into C major.

In the three cases referred to in connection with Examples 43, 45, and 48, however, in which the *second Subject* originally appeared in the less usual key, it appears in the original Tonic of the Movement in the *Recapitulation*.

An exceptional case of rare beauty may be instanced here, that of Mozart's Symphony in C major, No. 36, the first Allegro of which commences (Ex. 92). After the modu-

(92) *Allegro spiritoso.*

lating passage, which closes in G major, the *second Subject* enters in E minor, with indescribable *naïveté*, and after four bars in that key proceeds to G major, reiterating this order with changed instrumentation. (Ex. 93.) In the *Recapitulation* this appears in A minor and C major.

In those Movements in the Minor Mode in which the *second Subject* is in the so-called *relative Major key*, it is not infrequent in the *Recapitulation* for it to appear in the *Tonic Major*. Thus in Beethoven's Quartet for stringed instruments, Op. 18, No. 4, in C minor, commencing (Ex.

94), the *second Subject* is in E♭ major in the *first part*.

(94) *Allegro ma non tanto.*

(Ex. 95.) In the *Recapitulation* it appears in C major, the return to the Minor Mode being afterwards made by a

(95)

fine change in the *Coda*, and the Movement terminating in that Mode.

This is also the procedure in his Symphony in the same key, No. 5.

In the first Movement of the Sonata Op. 57 (see Ex. 66), this is likewise the plan. Also in the Pianoforte and Violin Sonata in C minor, Op. 30, No. 2.

In the first Movement of his Symphony No. 9 (the *Choral*) in D minor (Ex. 96), the *second Subject* appears

originally in B♭ major. (Ex. 97.) In the *Recapitulation* it

90   LECTURES ON MUSICAL ANALYSIS.   [LECT.

is taken in D major, a change of key, but not of Mode, nor, therefore, of sentiment.

In Mendelssohn's *Song without Words*, Book 1, No. 5, in F♯ minor, which is a movement of the structure now under consideration, commencing (Ex. 98), the *second Subject* is

in A major in the first part (Ex. 99), and in the *Tonic Major* in the *Recapitulation*.

This is also the order in the first Movement of Sterndale Bennett's Sonata in F minor, Op. 13, commencing (Ex. 100),

(100) *Moderato espressivo.*

the *second Subject* appearing first of all in A♭ major (Ex. 101), and in the *Recapitulation* in F major.

(101) *Cantabile.*

In the last Movement of the same Sonata, in his *Romance* in G minor, Op. 14, No. 3, in the last Movement of his *Fantasia*, Op. 16, and in other works of his, the same plan is pursued.

This is also Weber's method in his Sonatas in D minor, Op. 49, and E minor, Op. 70. Also Schumann's in his Sonata in G minor, Op. 22.

But in the instances above quoted from Haydn's Sonatas Nos. 13 and 23, and Mozart's Sonatas Nos. 8 and 14, a new sentiment is imparted by the presentation of the *second Subject* in the Minor Mode in the *Recapitulation*. This is also the case in Haydn's Sonata in E minor, No. 33. And with Mozart this is the usual method, in all cases with indescribable change of impression, and inviting attention to the harmonizing under new conditions. The first and last Movements of his Symphony in G minor, No. 40, are both on this plan. The *Finale* is especially to be quoted, on account of a modification, as well as the change of Mode in the *second Subject*, on its recurrence. (Ex. 102, 103.)

(102) *Allegro assai.*

In the first Movement of Beethoven's Op. 13, that portion of the *second Subject* which is in E♭ minor (see Ex. 68) enters in F minor in the *Recapitulation*, followed by C minor.

In all the cases referred to above, in which the *second Subject* of a Minor Movement appears in the first instance in the *Minor key* of the *Dominant*, it appears in the *Recapitulation* in the *Tonic Minor*.

In the first Movement of Beethoven's Sonata in A minor, for pianoforte and violin, Op. 47 (dedicated to Kreutzer), the *second Subject* is partly in E major and partly in E minor, and in the *Recapitulation*, correspondingly, is in A minor and A major.

With all these varieties of method and order, however, the important essentials are observed—*key-relationship* and *contrast* between the two principal Subjects.

LECTURE V.

THE INTRODUCTION PREFIXED TO SOME MOVEMENTS. SOMETIMES ONLY A PREFIX. IN MANY CASES ANTICIPATORY. EXAMPLES FROM BEETHOVEN, MENDELSSOHN, AND MOZART. ALLEGED GRAMMATICAL IRREGULARITIES IN THE INTRODUCTION TO MOZART'S SIXTH QUARTET. HOW TO VIEW SUCH INFRACTIONS OF RULE IN WORKS OF GENIUS.

V.

HAVING considered the material of which a Movement of development consists, both in its original presentation and in its recapitulatory or retrospective form, it will be convenient, before proceeding to the development, or *working out* of that material, in the second part, to notice the *anticipatory working* which occurs, in some compositions, in the INTRODUCTION, generally in slow time, to the quicker Movement. Sometimes this is simply a prefix, without any direct connection with or bearing on the Movement which it precedes, merely ushering it in as a preamble. In other cases, however, it is anticipatory, presenting some germs of the succeeding Movement, towards which it works, and so links itself with it as an integral part. Of this latter method we have already had one brief example in the initial phrase of Beethoven's Sonata, Op. 31, No. 2 (see Ex. 71), which not only is used as a bass (see Ex. 72), but reappears during the Movement, both in its original *quasi* Recitative form, and also as a bass in the quick portions of the Movement.

Another instance from Beethoven is in the Sonata Op. 13 (the *Pathetic*), which commences with a slow *Introduction* (Ex. 104), the opening phrase of which constitutes an

H

important feature in the course of the Movement. The chord marked * would now-a-days be explained as the last inversion of the *Dominant Minor 13th*, Root G, resolving on the first inversion of *Tonic* harmony; or, perhaps, as a triple Suspension. This *Introduction* leads to the quick Movement, commencing (Ex. 105). The three divisions of the *second*

Subject, that is to say, the three ideas in E♭, are given in Examples 68, 69, 70, p. 72.

At the conclusion of the *first part*, this *Grave* recurs in G minor (Ex. 106); and in these four bars occurs one of

INTRODUCTION TO BEETHOVEN'S OP. 13.

the most wonderful enharmonic changes to be found in music, though by means familiar to all of you who have written exercises on the *Minor 9th*. The chord in Ex. 104, which I have explained, here recurs as the last inversion of the *Dominant Minor 13th* in G minor, Root D; and, in the third bar, the *Minor 9th* of bar 2 is changed in notation to that of the *Dominant Minor 9th* in E minor, Root B; and this leads, most naturally, after the unexpected change has been confirmed in the fourth bar, to the resumption of the *Allegro*, a phrase from which is taken in E minor: very remote from the original key. This, however, is interrupted by the entry, bar 4, of the first phrase of the *Introduction*, but in *even* notes, instead of dotted. Compare bars 1, 2 with bars 8, 9, 10.

After the *Recapitulation*, the peroration of the Movement is interrupted by yet another recurrence of the *Grave*, four bars of which lead to a concise abridgement of the *Allegro Subject*, and so to the termination of the Movement. Thus the *Introduction* is incorporated with the whole Movement.

To the Sonata Op. 111, of which the *second Subject* is

quoted in Ex. 79, p. 77, there is an *Introduction* (Ex. 107)

in which may perhaps be discerned foreshadowings of the succeeding *Allegro*. This passage (Ex. 108) may have the

germ of the phrase in Ex. 79 just referred to. Observe that in bar 3 * of Ex. 108 the A♮ should be B double flat, *Minor* 9*th* to A♭, proceeding to the harmony of D♭.

This passage (Ex. 109) also seems to be an indistinct

anticipation of this in the *Allegro*. (Ex. 110.) But the *Introduction* does not recur.

Beethoven's Sonata, Op. 81ª, "*Les Adieux, l'Absence, et le Retour*," opens with an *Introduction* commencing (Ex. 111),

which leads into the *Allegro* thus (Ex. 112). The initial *Lebewohl* phrase reappears in this *Allegro* in various guises,

102   LECTURES ON MUSICAL ANALYSIS.   [LECT.

and so does the fragmentary semiquaver passage in the last extract, which seems, in fact, like a broken and, in the highest part, inverse form of the *Lebewohl:* shall we say broken by the emotion of a "*Farewell*"? This, as the bass, with the semiquaver figure of Ex. 111 superposed, constitute the *first Subject* of the *Allegro*.

The *Lebewohl* phrase, with a dotted note to begin with, instead of in even notes, appears not only in the third and fourth bars of the bass of this *Subject*, but again in the transitional passage (Ex. 113); and then, in changed aspect,

as the *second Subject* (Ex. 114); and then again by *diminution*, in the imitational passage (Ex. 115), re-entering in semibreves for the repeat. As shown in the extract, *second time* bars lead to a presentation of the *Subject* in C minor, interrupted by the *Lebewohl* theme; and of alternations of these two themes, the *second part* is principally made up,

BEETHOVEN'S OP. 81ª.

(114)

passing through C minor, G minor, E♭ minor, G♭, and again through C minor to the return of the *Subject* in the original

(115)

key. A very lengthened *Coda* presents the *Lebewohl* theme in varied aspect. Firstly, in responsive manner (Ex. 116),

(116)

both in single notes and in thirds; then with a florid passage *under* it (Ex. 117); then with a similar (not identical)

(117)

passage *over* it. Later on occurs this presentation, daringly defying theoretical justification. (Ex. 118.) Then by *diminu-*

tion, followed by fragmentary presentation; and finally the theme in the bass with superposed quavers (Ex. 119), after

which the Movement terminates. So that, in this instance, both in sentiment and in structure, the *Introduction* is of immense importance, giving the initial idea of the Movement in simple, but not in crude or unshapen aspect. Indeed, in neither of these two Sonatas, Op. 13 and Op. 111, is the term *Introduction* applied by the composer.

In the Sonata Op. 53, however, the last Movement is preceded by an *Adagio Molto*, which is expressly termed *Introduzione*, and which foreshadows the *Subject* of the succeeding *Rondo*. This is, perhaps, somewhat remarkable, inasmuch as it is stated that this *Introduction* was written subsequently to the Sonata, which originally included the *Andante* in F, now known as Op. 35. This, however, was

106   LECTURES ON MUSICAL ANALYSIS.   [LECT.

found to render the Sonata too long, and the *Introduction* we are now considering was substituted. The foreshadowing of the *Rondo* consists simply in the repeated notes in the second bar (Ex. 120), which recur many times, and, finally,

seem to reach their climax in the opening of the *Rondo* (Ex. 121), and subsequently have still greater reiteration. (Ex. 122.)

A beautiful instance of an *Introduction* suggestive of and gradually working towards the *Subject* of the succeeding Movement may be cited from Dussek's Sonata, "*The Farewell*," Op. 44. The *Introduction* opens thus (Ex. 123), and, after

the figure first announced in the bass has been many times repeated in varied guise, the following passage concludes the *Introduction* (Ex. 124), presenting the figure in shorter notes, and so preparing for its appearance, in the *Major mode*,

108   LECTURES ON MUSICAL ANALYSIS.   [LECT.

in the *Subject* of the *Allegro Moderato*. It seems thus to emerge from mist into sunshine.

Mendelssohn's "*Scotch*" Symphony, referred to in the last Lecture, opens with an *Introduction* commencing (Ex. 125), which seems anticipatory of the *Subject* of the succeeding Movement. See Example 77.

The *Introduction* of Beethoven's Seventh Symphony, commencing (Ex. 126), begins somewhat definitely to herald the

(126) *Poco sostenuto.*

opening of the *Vivace* in this passage. (Ex. 127.) The re-

peated notes ultimately lead into the *Subject* of the *Vivace* thus (Ex. 128).

In all these cases, however, the *Introduction* works *towards* the succeeding Movement: does not work *out* the *Subjects* as the *Free Fantasia* does. The *Introduction* may be said to furnish the *protoplasm* from which the *Subject* of the

110   LECTURES ON MUSICAL ANALYSIS.   [LECT.

quick Movement is *evolved;* whereas the *second part* of the Movement is the evolution of the material in the *first part.* The *Introduction* often seems like a *quest:* the *Subject* of the succeeding Movement like satisfaction. When one arrives at the *Allegro* of Beethoven's Fourth Symphony after the *Introduction* (for example), one feels inclined to exclaim "*Eureka!*"

In the larger number of cases the connection between the *Introduction* and the succeeding Movement is æsthetic, poetical, I might almost say, narrative rather than structural; and, therefore, comes less within our present scope of *analysis.*

There is one *Introduction* to which I may refer, the somewhat recondite harmony of which renders doubly welcome the charming simplicity of the *Allegro Subject* to which it leads. It is that of Mozart's String Quartet, No. 6. I quote it especially because its opening has scandalized some v.] INTRODUCTION TO MOZART'S QUARTET IN C. 111

musical grammarians. (Ex. 129.) Firstly, there is the *false relation* between A♭ in the viola and A♮ in the first violin, in the first two bars, recurring in the fifth and sixth bars between G♭ and G♮. But, though undoubtedly somewhat startling on first hearing, there is no real *false relation* of

keys, only the technical one of *notes*. And, being instrumental music, there is no difficulty, as in vocal music, in the production of the A♮ and G♮. Secondly, there are the consecutive seconds between the violoncello and the second violin, bars 2 and 3, and 6 and 7, which are uncompromisingly forbidden by some grammarians, and certainly to be avoided by students, who rarely—and, if at all, generally by accident —use exceptional progressions in the right place, and, intelligently, to enhance the effect: more frequently to escape from a difficulty. In the case before us, however, the C♯ is an *accented unessential* note, *auxiliary* to the D, which is the real harmony note. The same analysis applies to the B in bar 7. In these two phrases of four bars each, it is interesting to observe, in connection with the close imitation between the viola and the second violin, how the F♯, in the first phrase, and the E in the second phrase, both of them *essential* notes, are thus answered respectively by the C♯ and the B, both of them *auxiliary* or *unessential* notes of strongly-marked power. The prosecution of the *design* here is so evident, that we feel ourselves in the hands of a master and a genius, whose prerogative and whose power it is to pursue his course, not defiantly, but majestically independent of verbal rules. Do not mistake me. I am not apologizing, extenuating, palliating: Mozart's design and workmanship need no vindication of the kind. Moreover, I should not undertake the task for Mozart, any more than I do for you when you, in your exercises, infringe rules, or write ungrammatically. Neither am I questioning the excellence of the rules, nor throwing any stupid charge of pedantry upon them. Those who will not submit to discipline, to gain power, do this: not others. Speaking generally, the rules given to you are concrete expressions of sound principles, and should be rigidly observed. Nor am I asserting that a genius may write bad music, bad progressions, and that we are to

I

condone his offence out of consideration for his otherwise beautiful work. But I am contending that a genius and a master, like Mozart, may fairly claim, and unquestionably does generally justify that claim, to know and perceive when the principle involved in an axiomatic rule is, or is not, violated by a technical infringement of that rule.

The figure of ascending quavers, in the opening imitational passage of this *Introduction*, appears, as will be seen, in the *Subject* of the *Allegro*. This *Subject* is of so quiet a character as almost to require an *Introduction*, a remark which applies to other works—such, for example, as the first Movement of Mozart's Symphonies, No. 38, in D, and No. 39, in E♭.

Such daring passages as this *Introduction* need judging in their entirety, and with a comprehensive view of their design. Therefore, however startling on a first hearing, the reason and meaning of them can be understood, and subsequently be quite intelligible and acceptable. The structural and æsthetic design here is manifest: the presentation of the *motivo* firstly with the *Minor 6th*, A♭, answered by E♭, and then with the *Major 6th*, A♮. And similarly, in the succeeding passage, with the G♭, D♭, and G♮. No analysis is adequate which does not have regard to this design; which, however, though it may be technically *stated*, can only be *felt* poetically.

LECTURE VI.

SECOND PART, OR FREE FANTASIA. TEST OF A COMPOSER'S STRENGTH AND SCHOLARSHIP. FANCY TO BE REGULATED. SOME MOVEMENTS WITH LITTLE OR NO WORKING. SOME HAVE AN EPISODE IN THE SECOND PART. EXAMPLES FROM MOZART AND BEETHOVEN. MODULATION. FRAGMENTARY WORKING. EXAMPLES FROM HAYDN. REMARKS ON HIS PIANOFORTE (OR HARPSICHORD) MUSIC. HOW TO JUDGE MUSIC. METHODS OF WORKING SUMMARIZED. EXAMPLE OF CONSECUTIVE FIFTHS FROM BEETHOVEN.

VI.

WE now come to the *second part* of a Movement in Sonata form : not to be confounded with the *second Subject*. This *second part*, also called the *Free Fantasia*, consists of the *working* of the material in the *first part*, like the development of the plot in a novel or drama : bringing about incidents, relationships, involvements, entanglements, which were not expected as the characters were introduced. The *second part* has to present the *Subjects* in new aspects, and so exhibit their suggestiveness, power, and mutual relations. Music is pre-eminent among the fine arts for fertility of resource in this respect. In this power of working—involving capacity for foresight, contrivance, sustained thinking, design —lies very largely the mark of a great, masterly composer. We see in this part of a composer's work whether he apprehends the true power of music beyond its sensuousness, and the extent of his acquired musicianship, his command of the grammar of music, its logic, rhetoric, and structural devices. Weakness is discovered here if anywhere, and weak, imperfectly trained composers often decry the structure which requires this power, as pedantic or effete. It is easier for them to add to the number of unconnected, inconsequent themes in the Movement, and so to attain a certain length, than to *develop* a small number with power, coherence, consecution, and unity. Therefore they write fugitive pieces without any pretence to the structure that we are considering;

or, in larger pieces, seek to cover their lack of design by titles that seem to imply more free, unfettered imaginative play.

This *Free Fantasia*, as the *second part* is called, is that in which the composer is free to follow his own fancy: hence the term. Of course he is so all through, only that it is an accepted plan of the Movement that we are talking about that there shall be *first* and *second Subjects*, in certain related keys, and so on, as I have explained. But in the *second part* there is no such conventional understanding: the composer is free to modulate into what keys he pleases, within certain reasonable limits, and either to introduce new matter, new ideas or subjects, or to *work* any portion or portions of the material of the *first part* that may seem best for the purpose, and to work it in any of the various ways that musicians have at command. And it is about these ways or methods of working that I am now going to speak. Remember one thing, however: if *Free Fantasia* is the part where a composer gives free play to his fancy, it must not be thought that to be *fanciful* is to be *fantastic*. A true composer has not only fancy, but also knowledge, skill, and judgment; and these, disciplined and at ready command, combine to regulate and direct the exercise of his fancy. Fancy, imagination, must not be the only faculty brought into play in musical composition, any more than in other arts.

In some Movements by Haydn, Mozart, and other composers, the *second part*, from the double bar to the return of the *first Subject*, has no working, strictly so called, in any of the methods that I am going to describe and illustrate to you, nor even any modulation, but simply some connecting matter, following naturally upon and in keeping with the *first part*, mainly transitional, leading back to the original key and *Subject*.

This is the case in the first Movement of Mozart's Sonata No. 5, quoted at page 7, in which the *second part*, of eighteen bars length, has only the slightest reference to the *first part*, and nothing to be called real working. The same may be said of the twenty-nine bars which form the *second part* of the first Movement of his Sonata No. 10, commencing (Ex. 130), as also of the last Movement (which is in first

(130) *Allegro moderato.*

Movement form) of the same Sonata. In both cases, in fact, new matter is introduced: that in this last Movement being really a new *Subject* as an *Episode* (meaning a story introduced into another), prior to the return. This absence of working in certain of Mozart's Sonatas was not, we may be quite sure, from any lack of power or resource in the greatest writer of his time, but from the absence of pedantry, and the untrammelled sense of fitness which characterized him. The introduction of an episodical *Subject*, as in this case, is only an instance of his exuberant wealth of melodic resource. Similar *Episodes* occur in the first Movement of his Sonata in F, No. 12, and in No. 17 in the same key.

In Beethoven's Sonata Op. 14, No. 1, referred to at page 20, *et seq.*, the *second part* consists largely of an *Episode* (Ex. 131) of an impassioned character, between two quiet

passages founded on the quiet *first Subject*. In the Sonata Op. 10, No. 2, also, there is an *Episode* in the *second part*, commencing (Ex. 132).

In this same Sonata, moreover, we have an instance of the taking of a slight fragment or figure from the *first part*, as a starting-point, or catch-word, so to speak, as the suggestion for a little course of changes of harmony, or rapid modulations, passing through several keys. Thus the three octaves with which the *first part* of the Sonata before us terminated, are simply taken in the harmony of A (Ex. 133),

VI.] SECOND PART: FIGURE WORKING. 121

vague, but sufficient to serve as dominant to D minor; and then, on this simple figure, firstly as bass, and afterwards as upper part, is formed a triplet passage, leading to the aforementioned *Episode*, followed by a recurrence of this figure, in B flat, &c., and the return to the *Subject*, in D major, as mentioned in Lecture IV.

This kind of procedure is adopted in Mozart's Sonata No. 16, quoted in Examples 9 and 10. The *first part* terminates thus, in G major. (Ex. 134.) The semiquaver figure, in

G minor, opens the *second part;* and, alternating with scale passages, ascending and descending, drawn from the *first*

part, bars 5 to 10, passing through D minor and A minor, constitutes the whole of that *second part*, returning to the original *Subject*, though not in the original *key* of C, but of F major. See Lecture IV.

Again, in his Sonata No. 9, in D, commencing (Ex. 135),

(135) *Allegro con spirito.*

&c.

this phrase forms part of the *second Subject*. (Ex. 136.)

(136)

&c.

The two slurred quavers give the suggestion for the termination of the *first part*, thus (Ex. 137, bars 1, 2), and, upon

(137)

this apparently slight basis, an imitational passage is commenced, for the opening of the *second part* (bars 3, 4),

VI.] SECOND PART: FRAGMENT WORKING. 123

extending over sixteen bars, followed by other matter drawn from the *first part*. Quite exceptionally, the *second Subject* in the original key of the Movement occurs *before* the *first Subject* so reappears.

In fact, many *second parts* are formed simply on fragments of the *first part*, not worked in any contrapuntal, or what might seem *scholastic* way, but taken either in reiteration, or in alternation with one another, or merely like little reminiscences of the *first part*, in connection with modulations into some of the related keys. Modulation is one of the chief features in *second parts* that are at all lengthy or elaborate; but then it must be in conjunction with other treatment of the *Subjects*. Mere change of key, and giving the same idea in just the same form as at first, is a very poor way of eking out the Movement, and making up for lack of constructive skill.

Notice how, in Beethoven's Op. 49, No. 1, in G minor (see Ex. 64)—so concise a Movement, but so beautifully turned, so gracefully rounded, and all because so tenderly felt—the short *second part* is entirely made up of two fragments: one, the first phrase of the *second Subject*, the other the little termination at bars 23, 24, with a slight reminiscence of bar 14 and a diminution of bar 13. (Ex. 138.)

Some *second parts* commence with the *first Subject* in the

(138) See 2nd Subject, Ex. 64, p. 65.

key in which the *first part* has terminated, and an inexperienced listener might think that it was all to come over again in the new key. But here comes occasion for the skill of the composer—to perceive when and how to break off, to diverge by an interrupted cadence, or by some other by-path. Interrupted cadences, indeed, are most important features in this continuous, but also fragmentary and modulatory working. And, as with interrupted cadences, so with prolongation of phrases, by which cadences are deferred, or altogether averted, and modulation introduced.

Thus, Haydn's Sonata in E, No. 25, commences with this *Subject*. (Ex. 139.) The *second part* opens in like manner, in the key of the Dominant. (Ex. 140.) But, by prolongation in bar 4, the half-close in C♯ minor is effected, and in that key there follows a somewhat lengthened passage.

In Mozart's Sonata No. 8, in A minor, quoted in Examples 53, 54, 88, and 89, the *second part* opens with the original

VI.] SECOND PARTS: HAYDN AND MOZART. 125

first Subject in C major (Ex. 141); but a diversion is effected in the fourth bar, seemingly, according to the notation, to

the key of F. Here, however, occurs a somewhat anomalous oscillation, for at the sixth bar the D♭, minor 9th to C, dominant of F, is enharmonically changed to C♯, which changes the root to A, and seems to indicate a diversion to

D minor. Instead of resolving to that harmony, however, return is immediately made to the dominant harmony in F, rendering quite nugatory and inexplicable the previous enharmonic change. And then, most beautifully, this dominant 7th in F, bar 7, is in bar 8 enharmonically changed to the augmented (German) 6th in the key of E minor, and the remainder of the *second part* consists mainly of working, founded on the *first Subject*, of this figure with Suspensions forming the last four bars of the extract, passing through the keys of E minor, A minor, D minor, &c.; so leading back to the original key and *Subject*, and continuing as indicated in connection with Fig. 89.

Haydn's Sonata No. 13, quoted in Ex. 49, has a *second part* which is instructive for its modulations in conjunction with fragmentary working. The *first part* having closed in D major, the *second part* opens with a modulation to E minor, founded on the *first Subject*, which is then taken in that key, but breaks off by an *interrupted cadence* (Ex. 142,

(142)

Int. Cad.

bar 1), which, by a prolongation of the semiquaver figure, leads through A major to F♯ minor, in which key a half-close is made. The *Subject* is then commenced in that key, and, by a reiteration of the figure in bar 10 of Ex. 49, a progression through C♯ minor, with an enharmonic *implied*, not expressed (the F double sharp, bar 10, being treated as G♮), the original key of B minor is reached.

The short, strong *second part* of Mozart's Sonata in C minor, quoted in Examples 55, 56, 57, 58, 90, and 91, is founded almost entirely on the *first Subject* figure as given in the first two bars of Ex. 56, with a parenthesis of that portion of the *second Subject* which forms the succeeding four bars of the same Example. F minor and G minor are the keys passed through, leading back to the original key. The following figured bass represents the very simple succession of harmonies on which this vigorous working proceeds. (Ex. 143.)

Although I point out to you any instances of enharmonic or exceptional modulation, especially where the notation is not strictly accurate or explicit, either from motives of expediency, saving of accidentals, or the like, yet it is of by far the greater importance for you to observe the masterly manner in which the more ordinary and natural modulations are effected by these great masters whose works I am helping you to analyse. Speaking generally, the modulations in the *second parts* of these Movements are, however "free" the "Fantasia," *natural*, that is, into related, keys, allied to the original key, rather than *extraneous*, or into *foreign* keys. It is with a view of habituating you to the observance and admiration of this masterly naturalness in great music that I draw so many of my examples from the older composers,

K

such as Haydn and Mozart. To "Papa Haydn," as his countrymen have delighted to call him, "the father of modern instrumental music," we are indebted for the perfecting of the very form, Sonata or Symphonic, which we have been considering: the *Duplex* or *Binary*, some have called it. In listening to his pianoforte music, however, you must not judge of it in comparison with that of more recent times. I am not speaking apologetically, as though the beauty of the old master's music could be eclipsed or outshone by the more highly-wrought, more elaborated, more brilliant, more full, sensuous, and, in one sense, effective music of the later periods. It is yourselves that you will rob if you expect these features in music of the early period, instead of looking for the essential, integral elements which constitute real musical worth, as distinguished from accessories. Remember that the instruments and the players written for by Haydn and Mozart were not our modern ones, and that pianoforte music was almost in its infancy. The very first published Sonata of Beethoven's, Op. 2, dedicated to Haydn, his master, was not produced till 1796, when Haydn was sixty-four years of age, and Mozart's Sonatas and all his other works had been composed—he, alas! having been dead five years. I cannot do you much better service than this of helping you to dissociate the *sense* from the *sensational*, and the *essentials* from the *accidents*, in music as in other arts. The arrangement, manner of writing, or setting forth of ideas for the pianoforte, as for other instruments, is fuller now than formerly; but that does not bring more fulness of idea, of thought, of invention. Of course you will not think that I am advocating any stupid deprecation of advance in methods of presentation, in accordance with additional appliances, and more extended executive skill. But I am desirous that you shall not take these for more than they are worth. The value of gold does not consist in its glitter. "Fine feathers make fine birds;" but fine *arpeggios*, brilliant passages, these do not make fine music. It is not the fulness of an orchestral work, or the amount of brass in it, admirable as these may be, which constitute fine instrumentation; but, rather, the giving individuality to the separate instrumental parts, according to the character and capacity of each instrument. This may seem somewhat a digression, but it has much to do with the general principles on which music should be judged, the way of intelligently listening to it, and of analysing it.

Thus far, however, I have said very little about the methods of working, having referred to some Movements in which there is but little, to some in which there is episodical matter introduced in the *second part*. I have also so far anticipated myself as to glance at a few easily understood instances of working. It is time, however, that I speak more systematically about the *working of Subjects* in music, which is a matter of almost boundless interest; so varied are the methods in which it may be done, and such scope does it afford for the exercise of genius, ingenuity, and scholarship. So diverse are musical *Subjects* in their suggestiveness, that only a general classification of the ways in which they may be treated can be given, with such illustrations as may help you in listening to the works of the great masters with watchful interest and intelligent discernment.

You will be prepared to hear that all the various devices, and all the theoretical knowledge, about which you are told in your class lessons, are brought into practical application in the working of *Subjects*. Only it must be remembered and observed that these devices have to be selected and used with discrimination, appropriately to the *Subjects* that have to be worked. To misuse or over-use them becomes pedantic. That nice sense of fitness is required which the

Greeks expressed by their proverb, "Do nothing too much." I may so far anticipate the subject of another Lecture as to say that a FUGUE is the very concentration of working devices, and is understood to consist of continuous, almost unbroken working, though even in this form of composition it is quite possible to infringe the spirit of the Greek proverb. And, in a CANON, the working is *stringent*, not *optional*, when once the particular form of Canon is determined upon. In such compositions, fancy, imagination, genius, must manifest themselves within the prescribed and accepted restrictions, not in breaking through them, as is sometimes said to be, and at certain times undoubtedly is, the prerogative of genius. A Fugue writer must manifest his genius in his *Subject:* that should be *multum in parvo*, especially when enriched by its *counter-Subject*, and then developed into the *Exposition*, which is as the egg from which the whole Fugue is to be hatched.

But in the freer plans of composition, such as the Sonata Movements which we have been considering, while opportunity may occur for the use of any or all of the various working devices which are closely packed in a Fugue, they are brought into requisition entirely at the fancy or judgment of the composer. In speaking of the working in the *second part* of a Sonata Movement, I shall inevitably touch on some of the same processes as those which appertain to Fugue structure.

To enumerate, then, some of the methods of working *Subjects*, or presenting them in various aspects, there is, firstly, the presenting the same *melody* with different *harmony*, or the same *harmony* with different *melody*, or the same harmony and melody, either in different positions, or with such ornamentation, embellishment, and diversity as may be effected by passing notes, suspensions, and the like. Closely allied with these methods is that of presenting a *Subject*, or part of it, in contrapuntal form, with contrapuntal adjunct, which has originally appeared in simpler guise. This, again, as many of you will understand, may lead to the placing that in an inner part, or in the lowest part, which has been the highest part: technically termed *inverting* the parts. Here, of course, comes in the true use of *double-counterpoint*. And, still further, one of the principal methods is *fragmentary working*, such as the few instances I have given you: taking some one or more portions or *figures* of a *Subject*, and working them apart from their original context, or with that context in changed order: alternating such fragments, or bringing them together, *stretto* fashion (see Lecture XIV). Or it may be that portions, fragments, of different *Subjects*, the first and the second, or figures taken from the connecting or supplementary matter, are thus alernated or combined. The *Subjects*, or fragments of them, may be taken, moreover, by *inverse motion*, or by *augmentation*, or by *diminution*—these last two terms meaning in notes of *greater* or *less* length, respectively, than in their original presentation. And the various imitational devices, fugal, canonic, or free, may be used. In fact, the *second part* of such a Movement as we are considering may be regarded as an argument on the *theses* laid down in the *first part*; now this, now that, being most prominently urged and expounded in its various salient or strong points. Or it may be likened to a general conversation or discussion about certain events which have taken place: the different incidents being recalled and dilated upon in various ways, according to the perceptions, memories, and impressions of different spectators, or, it may be, actors, in such supposed events. This general summary may serve to awaken your interest, and guide you as to what to look out for, when the working or development begins.

Again I urge that mere transposition of any *Subject* to another key, without any change of presentation, is a poor pretence, and indicates weakness. There must at least be some change of accompaniment or of rhythm in conjunction with the change of key. Rhythmical devices, such as contraction, extension, overlapping, and other forms of what is termed *broken rhythm*, are among the resources for evading squareness, tameness, and monotony. Broken rhythm was a strong point with Haydn.

You will be prepared now for examples of these various devices, which I will introduce and explain in the next Lecture.

In the Sonata Op. 14, No. 1, of Beethoven, which I have referred to in this and in other Lectures, there is in one portion of the *second Subject*, both times of its presentation, an instance of consecutive fifths—whether by oversight or not I cannot say. Here it is. (Ex. 144.)

LECTURE VII.

SECOND PART OF MOVEMENT OF DEVELOPMENT, *continued.* MANY SLOW MOVEMENTS AND FINAL MOVEMENTS OF THIS STRUCTURE. MODULATION AN IMPORTANT FEATURE, IN CONJUNCTION WITH WORKING. MOST FREQUENTLY NATURAL, THOUGH SOMETIMES EXTRANEOUS. COMPARISON OF MODULATIONS IN MOVEMENTS IN E FLAT. SIMILAR COMPARISON IN MOVEMENTS IN G MINOR. TRUE VIEWS ABOUT RELATED KEYS, AND NATURAL AND EXTRANEOUS MODULATION. IMITATION: FUGAL, CANONIC, FREE. EXAMPLES OF IMITATIONAL WORKING FROM HAYDN, MOZART, AND BEETHOVEN.

VII.

BEFORE entering still further upon the construction of *second parts* of movements of continuity, I may as well say that many *slow movements* of Sonatas, Symphonies, &c. are of this plan, as also are many *final movements;* so that our range is enlarged for the analysis which is occupying us. Moreover, the *Minuet,* or *Scherzo,* which in many cases follows, occasionally precedes, the slow movement, affords example of this same structure on a small scale, being like a compact little first movement, in order of keys and subjects. To this latter kind of movement, however, I shall recur in a future Lecture; but we may well include, in our present survey, some slow movements of continuity, and some final movements; the slow movement generally following, with welcome repose, the first *Allegro* movement, and the *Minuet* or *Scherzo,* with shorter rhythms and lighter character, affording relief, after the tension of those two preceding movements.

I have said that *modulation,* in conjunction with and as part of the development of the subjects, is of the very nature of a so-called *Free Fantasia.* I have also said that in by far the larger number of works by the great masters, the modulations in the second part are *natural* rather than extraneous. This has to do with the *congruity* of thought; *extraneous* modulation having somewhat of the character which, in a *novel* or a *drama,* is termed *improbability,* or *startling situation.* Of course such incidents *may* occur, though lacking the verisimilitude of real life. And by no means should *extraneous* modulation be "tabooed" as necessarily irregular. But life may be very interesting without frequent surprises. And we must hardly take the recent adage that "nothing is certain but the unexpected" which does not describe real life, as applicable to *Art*, and as justifying any notion that, in a work of Art, nothing is good, or at least *original*, but the unexpected.

Let it again be observed and remembered that the modulations in a second part enter into the course of thought, are essentials of the development, and effected in conjunction with the working.

It may be interesting to compare the courses of modulation in different works. Take, as examples, several movements in the key of E♭ major. First of all, Haydn's Sonata No. 29, quoted in Examples 26 and 27, after the close of the first part of the first movement, in B♭, commences the second part in C minor, very briefly; and then passes to A♭, and, through C minor, returns to the original key. His Sonata No. 32, quoted in Examples 28, 29, and 30, commences the second part in B♭, passes through C minor, A♭, F minor, slightly touching on D♭ and B♭ minor, and returns to the original key. No. 34, dedicated to Mrs. Bartolozzi, the largest of his Sonatas, commencing (Ex. 145), has a much

(145) *Allegro.*

more discursive *Free Fantasia;* modulating through C major,

F major (very briefly), G minor, C minor, F minor, A♭, C minor again, E major (by a sudden transition), A major, B minor, and, enharmonically, back to the original key. To this enharmonic modulation I must draw your special attention. The following phrase from the *first Subject* (Ex. 146), afterwards, in the first part, taken with the

melody under the accompaniment (Ex. 147), is here also so

taken and prolonged (Ex. 148); the dominant 7th in B is, by an *implied* enharmonic, treated as an Augmented 6th on G♭, with, as is now considered, the roots F and C, in the

key of B♭; by the dominant 7th in which key it passes to the root B♭, with a 7th, dominant to E♭, the original key.

Not only is there the above-named modulation, or transition, to E♮ major, in the second part of this first movement, but the succeeding Adagio, also, is in the same key, unrelated to that of the first and last movements, E♭ major.

The first Allegro of Mozart's Symphony in E♭, No 39, modulates, in the second part, to A♭ and C minor, slightly touching on F minor and G minor. In the last movement, which is also of the plan that we have all along been considering, after the first part has, as usual, finished in the Dominant, B♭, after a bold unison passage on the dominant of C minor, the original subject is taken in A♭, followed by working through E major, E minor, C major, C minor, G minor, D minor, and back to E♭.

The second part of the first movement of Beethoven's Sonata Op. 7, in this same key, E♭, modulates, after the close of the first part in the Dominant, to C minor, A♭,

F minor, G minor, A minor, D minor, and back to E♭. The modulation from G minor to A minor is by an implied enharmonic (Ex. 149); the D$\sharp\sharp$ in bar 4 being E♭ in

(149)

relation to the key quitted, root D; the change to D$\sharp\sharp$ giving the root B, super-tonic of A minor. The modulations from D minor to E♭, in this Sonata, and in the last movement of Mozart's Symphony, just noticed, are worth comparing. In the Symphony (Ex. 150) the B♮ is, by implication,

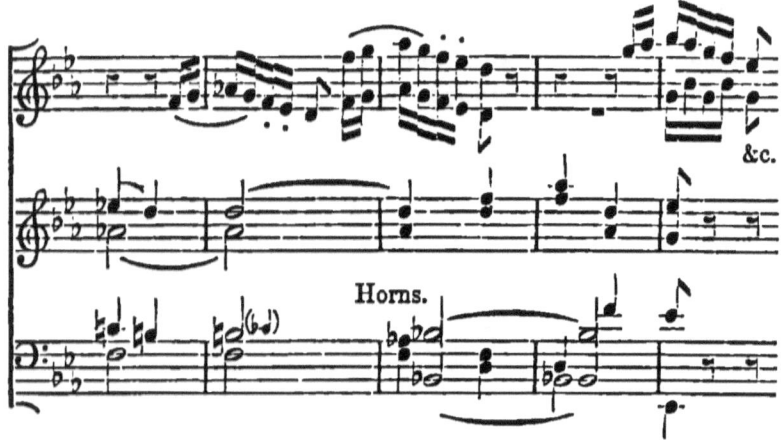

enharmonically changed to C♭, minor 9th to the dominant of E♭. In the Sonata, the first inversion of the dominant 7th in E♭ (Ex. 151), bars 3, 4, is the enharmonic of the

(151)

first inversion of the Augmented (German) 6th on B♮, minor 6th of the scale of D minor.

The first movement of Beethoven's Sonata in the same key, Op. 31, No. 3 (see Examples 16, 17, 18, 84), modulates, in the second part, through C major, F major, F minor, and then returns to E♭ as shown in Ex. 84. The second part of the last movement of the same Sonata passes through G♭, B minor (by enharmonically changing G♭ to F♯), C minor, C major, F minor, A♭, and then to E♭.

Beethoven's Sonata Op. 81 *a* (see Examples 111 to 119

inclusive) modulates, in the second part of the first *Allegro*, through C minor (transiently), B♭ minor, G minor, E♭ minor, G♭, C minor (by enharmonic of C♭ and B♮), and then to the original key, but without any close in either of these keys. The second part of the last movement of the same Sonata modulates through E♭ minor, D♭, G♭, all very transiently, to B major, G, C, A♭, and then to E♭.

This comparison of the modulations in nine movements in the same major key will suffice. Even where the modulations are extraneous, they are, for the most part, so naturally managed as to seem perfectly coherent, and not at all *un*-natural. And it is not a little remarkable that of all these works, that by Haydn, No. 34, is at least as discursive, extraneous, non-relative, as any of them; although it is sometimes thought that he is old-fashioned, conventional, and un-daring.

We will now, in the same way, compare several movements in G minor, and again will begin with Haydn. The Sonata No. 23, of which the two Subjects of the first movement are given in Examples 50, 51 (see also Ex. 87), is noteworthy for the structure of its second part, which, beginning in C minor, with the *first Subject*, does not continue even for the original four bars, but is interrupted by a *prolongation* (Ex. 152), during which the Arpeggio figure from the

first part is added, and a *diminution* of the passage at bar 5, semiquavers for quavers. This is reiterated in F minor, and, after two bars of reminiscence, the apparently unimportant termination at bar 12 of the first part is reiterated, plaintively, for three bars, in E flat and C minor. Then the *second Subject*, originally in the *Major Mode*, is introduced in C *minor*, but broken off in three bars. After a pause, a somewhat contrapuntal passage (Ex. 153), built on the *first*

(153)

Subject, touching on several keys, leads back beautifully to the original key. And all this compact working is within the compass of twenty-one bars! It might truly be termed a model second part, but that there must be equally suggestive and tractable material for working, ere it could be taken as a model.

Mozart's Quintet No. 3, for stringed instruments, commences thus (Ex. 154). The first part, having had a close

(154) *Allegro.*

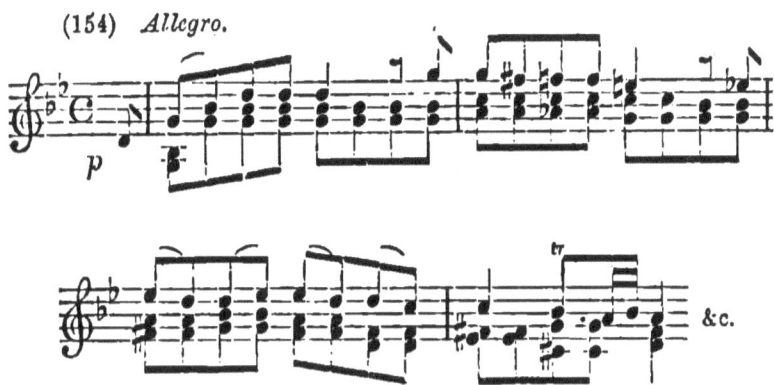

in B♭, has a short passage to lead back to the original key, for the repeat: then for the continuation to the second part, a reiteration of that passage, in C minor, in which key, however, there is no close, but a diversion to A♭, then to D♭, E♭ minor, F minor, all transiently, and back to G minor.

Mozart's Symphony in the same key, No. 40 (see Examples 102, 103), is remarkable for its modulations, as well as for every other characteristic of fine music, structural and emotional.

The first movement commences thus (Ex. 155); and

the first part, closing in B♭, has, similarly to the above

mentioned Quintet, a dominant chord in G minor, for the repeat (Ex. 156). The second part opens with the continuation of chords, bar 4, the G♯ giving the impression of A♭, minor 9th on G, but being here, by implication, enhar-

monically changed, and then, by another enharmonic, E♯ for F, the root is again changed from E to C♯, leading to the *first Subject* in the very remote key of F♯ minor. A beautifully delicate deviation from the original Subject by the B♮, bar 10, rendering the chord a fundamental (Supertonic) in its third inversion; resolving to the last inversion of the dominant 11th, bar 11, followed by first inversion of dominant 7th. The passage is reiterated sequentially, with A♯ instead of A♮, in like manner, bar 14, with the Subject as bass, so leading to E minor, through D minor, C major, B♭, and finally, by a dominant pedal passage, back to G minor, all with splendid imitational working. In this and other instances the mere enumeration of the keys passed into might give the impression of most erratic discursiveness ; but, partly by the transitoriness of some of these visits to remote keys, and partly by the sequential progression by which some of them are effected, as well as by the masterly and satisfactory harmonies and workings, this is not felt, as it would be if there were bungling, or if starts and closes were made in all these extraneous keys.

The last movement of the same Symphony opens thus (Ex. 157), and the first part closes in B♭. The second part

(157) *Allegro assai.*

is almost entirely constituted of imitational working of the Subject figure, just quoted. Opening with this bold passage (Ex. 158), remarkable for its rhythm, as well as for its harmonies, which are implied rather than expressed fully, the key of D minor is reached, and imitational working follows, on the dominant harmonies of C minor, E♭, C minor, G minor, D minor, A minor, E minor, B minor, F♯, reaching at last C♯ minor, in which a close is made, followed by this

MOZART'S SYMPHONY IN G MINOR

(158)

modulatory and imitational passage, to return to G minor (Ex. 159). There is no continuance in any one key throughout this *Free Fantasia*, which consists of a series of rapid transitions.

When we speak of *natural* and *extraneous* modulation, it is well to understand that other keys than those generally termed *the attendants* of any given key, ought to be reckoned as related to it. It is usual to call those five keys relative or attendant which have, respectively, the same signature as

the original key, and one more and one less flat or sharp. Thus, to G major, the so-called attendants are reckoned as D and C major, and E, B, and A minor. To this surely should be added, if addition it is to be termed, the Tonic minor, G minor. But, more than this, E flat major, having the note G in its *Tonic Triad*, and B major, with its *Tonic* in the *Triad* of G, should surely be included; in other words, the *Mediant* of the original key, and the key of which its *Tonic* is the *Mediant*. We have already seen, in Lecture III., that the key of the *Mediant* is that in which the *second Subject* of movements in the major mode is sometimes taken. And in Dussek's Sonata in G major, Op. 35, No. 2, the *second Subject*, which in the first part appeared in the Dominant, D, commences, in the *Recapitulation*, in E♭. The affinity between the keys in this relation to one another can hardly fail to be felt, apart from any acoustical considerations; and modulation to these keys should not be considered as *extraneous*, but as *natural*. It may with interest be observed, also, that whereas even a *natural* modulation may be so *un*-naturally made as to sound extraneous, so, on the other hand, modulation into remote keys may be so skilfully effected as to have no effect of incongruity, hardly of surprise. And, still further, that in a course of rapid passings through various keys, if there be no relationship between some of those keys and the original key, yet if they occur in congruous order, and if there be no *cadence* or *continuance* in the remote keys, the divergence from the natural course is scarcely felt. In many cases, of course, for dramatic or other purposes, sudden transitions are intended to arrest attention; but the remarks that I have been making have reference to modulations in a second part of a movement of continuity, of regular structure. Some speakers can with skill digress and with adroitness return to the main current of discourse. When a novice or tyro attempts this, the result generally is an impression of *rambling:* as is commonly said, "he does not seem to know what he is driving at."

Still further: in looking through such an enumeration of keys as some of those I have given, it may seem that there is an infringement of the very excellent rule that you have often heard from me—not to modulate into the same key twice in one movement. But this rule is not, in spirit, infringed when there is only a transient passage through, not a cadence in, the key in question.

I have repeatedly used the term *Imitational* in my allusions to the workings of Subjects. *Imitation*, as you know, is the progression of one part in the same manner as another part has progressed just previously; either in the same intervals, or in general form only. In a FUGUE, the Imitation is, in the first instance, of an entire phrase, or complete *Theme*, or *Subject*, in a manner defined by the rules appertaining to that form of composition, which, moreover, indicate certain modifications of exactitude in the Imitation. In a CANON, the Imitation, in the *Consequent* (as the imitating part is called), is not modified, but answers seconds by seconds, thirds by thirds, and so on. The imitation, however, may either be the reiteration of the same *notes* as those of the *Antecedent* (part imitated), Canon in the *unison*, or in the *octave;* or at any interval above or below. If the Canon be at certain intervals, the Imitation will be, though still exact as to *numerical* intervals, seconds for seconds, &c., yet not *strict*, but *free* as to the *quality* of those intervals; *minor* intervals answering *major* intervals, &c. I will not now enlarge on *Canonic* imitation; but, in connection with the matter of *Imitation*, as it concerns us in observing the working of Subjects, will further remind you that *Imitation* may be by *contrary* or *inverse motion: i. e.*

ascents for *descents*, and *vice versâ;* and by *retrograde motion*, from the end to the beginning—not much used, however. Also, *Imitation* may be by *Augmentation, i. e.* in *longer* notes than in the pattern; or, on the other hand, by *Diminution, i. e.* in *shorter* notes. I have dealt with the whole matter in my *Text-book;* but this summary may be useful as a reminder.

Apart from the strictly *scholastic* use of imitational devices, as in *Fugue* and *Canon*, the beauty of it, in free working, consists in the mutual activity and interweaving of parts which it induces; and in this respect it is a most important adjunct of fragmentary working. Fragmentary working so carried on is like an intelligent conversation on the details or bearings of certain propositions or events. Finished writing of this kind may be termed *scholarly* rather than scholastic.

Mozart's Sonata in F, No. 15, has various imitational devices. The *first Subject* commences (Ex. 160). One

imitational passage founded on this Subject is given in my *Text-book*, p. 177, Fig. 309. Another, drawn from the same figure, is (Ex. 161).

Then, the *second Subject* begins (Ex. 162), and this is

154 LECTURES ON MUSICAL ANALYSIS. [LECT.

worked by imitation in the octave (Ex. 163) and in the fifth (Ex. 164).

The following also (Ex. 165), drawn from the left-hand

passage of Ex. 162, after being worked above and below that triplet passage, is, in the *Recapitulation*, brought together with the *first Subject*, to which it makes an admirable *Counter-Subject*: there is no effort to fit it in, as is so often the case in second-rate works: no necessity for explanatory justification. (Ex 166.) In all these cases, observe that the

Imitation overlaps the part imitated; which, indeed, is of the very essence of vivid Imitation. There is no skill in one part *repeating* what another part has announced, when that anouncing part has finished, unless there be, as in the case of a *Fugue*, a Counterpoint to set it off. In these quoted passages, *Antecedent* and *Consequent* are brought together contrapuntally, after the manner of a *Stretto*, which we shall consider when analysing *Fugue* structure.

While considering this matchless Sonata, notice the following instance of an *Interrupted* Cadence (Ex. 167), and then how beautifully the scale passage is readjusted to the changed harmony, thus (Ex. 168)—a characteristic trait in Mozart's writing. And then, in the *Recapitulation*, the above passage is exquisitely prolonged, thus. (Ex. 169.)

156 LECTURES ON MUSICAL ANALYSIS. [LECT.

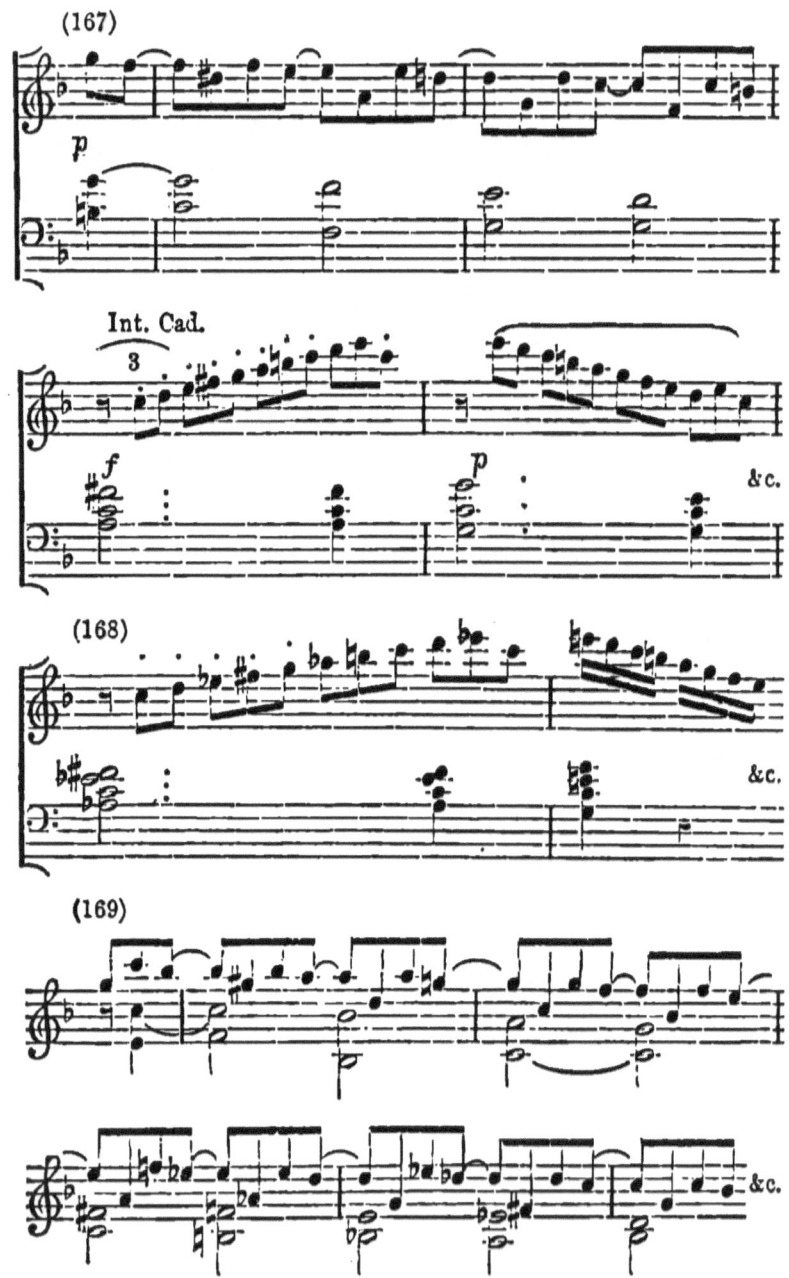

In Haydn's Sonata, No. 13, the first Movement of which is quoted in Examples 49 and 142, the Subject of the last Movement commences (Ex. 170); in itself of imitational

(170) *Presto.*

[musical notation]

character. In the second part these Imitations occur. (Examples 171, 172.)

In his Sonata in D, No. 17, the Subject of the last Movement commences (Ex. 173). The second part of this Subject

is imitational, thus. (Ex. 174.) Observe, however, the

consecutive 5ths, bars 4, 5. Further on this closer Imitation is taken. (Ex. 175.) Subsequently the inverse form of the

Subject is taken as its *Counterpoint*, and then that arrangement inverted. (Ex. 176.) Later on these forms occur.

(Examples 177, 178.) In these cases observe the different intervals at which the Imitations are introduced, and the slightness of the material which is so worked. When you see a Contrapuntist at play, you do not witness learned

160   LECTURES ON MUSICAL ANALYSIS.   [LECT.

trifling, but cheerful, even merry learning: there is all the difference. Many such instances might be adduced from the Symphonies and other works of Haydn.

The slow movement of Beethoven's Sonata Op. 22 (the first movement of which is considered in Lecture II.) invites study for the imitational structure of its second part, no less than for the exquisite beauty of the whole, with its long-drawn melodiousness and indescribable expressiveness. The *first Subject* commences thus (Ex. 179), and this furnishes the material for a beautiful *dialogue* in the second part,

&c.

giving the impression of two persons discussing or reminding one another of pleasant experiences: or, even more tenderly, assuring one another of mutual affection. But they progress while they converse: the modulation from C minor, in which the second part opens, proceeding through the Dominants of F minor, B♭, E♭, to A♭ minor, E♭ minor, in which a *half-close* is made, followed by the return to the primary key and *first Subject*. No *full-close* occurs in the second part. (Ex. 180.) In the *Recapitulation*, a noticeable point is that this passage in the first part, by which the modulation

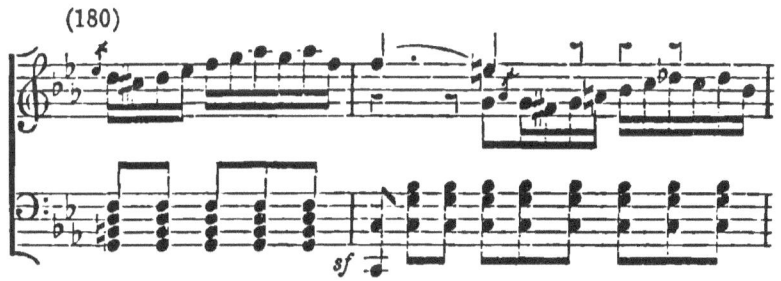

to the Dominant was effected (Ex. 181), is here (Ex. 182)

taken in the minor mode, and prolonged, passing through G♭, a cadence in that key, however, being interrupted, bar 4, and the *second Subject* then follows, with delightful freshness, in the original key of the Movement, E♭ major.

Beethoven's Sonata Op. 2, No. 2, after the opening quoted in Ex. 34, proceeds thus. (Ex. 183.) The first part closes in the Dominant, E *major*. The chord of E *minor* is then reiterated, and the *first Subject* is taken (Ex. 184) in C, an interrupted cadence leading to A♭, in which the Subject is worked. A *half-close* in F is reached, and then imitational working of the second figure in Ex. 183, leading through

(183)

164　LECTURES ON MUSICAL ANALYSIS.　[LECT.

(184)

D minor to A minor (Ex. 185), soon followed by the return to the Subject.

His Sonata No. 3 of the same *Opus*, quoted in Examples 36, 37, has a remarkable enharmonic passage in Arpeggio, in the second part, of which this (Ex. 186) is the outline,

leading to the Subject in the remote key of D *major*. This, however, is made the Dominant to G minor, which harmony being changed to *major* is made the Dominant to C *minor*, in which this bold imitational and syncopated passage, derived from a figure in the Subject (Ex. 187), is taken, and worked

through F minor, followed by a Pedal-bass passage on G, leading to the original key and Subject.

The first movement of Beethoven's Sonata Op. 111,

quoted in Examples 107, 108, 109, 110, has an imitational, almost fugal, passage, in the second part, the *first Subject* figure forming the counterpoint to its own augmentation, thus (Ex. 188).

Beethoven's Sonata in F minor, Op. 2, No. 1, has noticeable points of other kinds. The *first Subject* (Ex. 189) is in two bar-rhythm. The *second Subject*, beginning

at bar 20 (Ex. 190), in A flat *minor*, afterwards proceeds to the *major* mode. At the opening of the second part, great

relief is afforded by the three-bar rhythm presentation of the *first Subject*, in the *major* mode. (Ex. 191.) Then follows

the first section of the *second Subject*, in B flat minor and C minor, successively; this being then taken as the bass, a new aspect. (Ex. 192.) After this, a passage deriving its special point from *Syncopation* (Ex. 193), cross accent, leads,

(192)

(193)

after a passage on a dominant pedal, to a passage with suspensions, &c., returning to the Subject.

LECTURE VIII.

SECOND PART OF MOVEMENT OF DEVELOPMENT, *continued*. INVERSION OF PARTS. CONTRAPUNTAL TREATMENT. EXAMPLES FROM HAYDN'S AND MOZART'S SONATAS. RHYTHMICAL DEVICES, AVERTING SQUARENESS. CHANGED CHARACTER OF A THEME BY VARIED PRESENTATION. EXAMPLE FROM BEETHOVEN'S OP. 22. DOUBLE COUNTERPOINT. EXAMPLES FROM BEETHOVEN'S OP. 28. FUGAL WORKING. BEETHOVEN'S OP. 106. POWER OF IMITATIONAL DEVICES. MOZART'S DUET IN F. CONCERTED CHAMBER MUSIC. EXAMPLES FROM HAYDN'S AND MOZART'S QUARTETS, MOZART'S AND BEETHOVEN'S QUINTETS, AND BEETHOVEN'S SEPTET. GENERAL RESULT OF THIS SURVEY.

VIII.

ONE of the interesting methods of presenting musical themes in varied aspects is that of taking that which has been an upper, or the highest part, and placing it in an inner, or as the lowest part. More scope for this seems afforded in music for several voices or instruments; though how much may be done in this way on the pianoforte alone, let the Fugues of Bach, Handel, Mozart, and Mendelssohn exemplify. And we have seen how it may be done in non-fugal works; as, for example, in Examples 33, 37, 39, 52, &c.

Another example is furnished by Haydn's Sonata No. 30, of which the *first Subject* is given at page 6. The *second Subject* commences thus (Ex. 194).

(194)

After five bars, an unusual rhythm, this second section occurs (Ex. 195); the upper part being evidently evolved from the *first Subject*, and the lower figure of semiquavers being founded on the ascent of thirds which forms the left-hand part in Ex. 194; that, moreover, with its repeated

172   LECTURES ON MUSICAL ANALYSIS.   [LECT.

(195)

notes, having its origin apparently in the repeated notes of the *first Subject*.

Now observe that the *second part* opens with the *first Subject* as the lowest part (Ex. 196), and then the semi-

(196)

quaver figure of Ex. 195, bar 2, is introduced, and a modulation is made to B minor. This is followed by the same figure being superposed on that of the *first Subject*, being an inversion of the second section of the *second Subject* (see Ex. 195). Then comes a prolongation, by inverse movement, of the right-hand semiquaver figure in that second section, taken as the bass of a series of suspensions. After some Arpeggios, drawn from the first part, the return to the original key is effected.

Another example of similar contrapuntal treatment—for it is this varied turning to account of simple phrases which contrapuntal studies suggest, as you are often reminded in class—may be adduced from Haydn's Sonata No. 32, already quoted in Examples 28 and 29. The first part closing with a *Codetta*, a fragment from that Codetta is then made the theme for contrapuntal treatment. (Ex. 197.)

The last Movement of Mozart's Sonata in C, No. 1,

(197)

commences (Ex. 198). This figure is inverted and embel-

lished in the second part, in conjunction with modulation, as I have told you is usual with Subject working. (Ex. 199.)

The *second Subject* commences (Ex. 200). This likewise is inverted in the second part. (Ex. 201.)

These instances, and many like them, are undoubtedly very *simple*, almost self-evident, as is often thought of such cases: hardly to be termed *contrapuntal* working, in the sense of combining independent parts, each having an individuality. But it is contrapuntal training, which was *the* training in the old times, that suggests such working, engendering the mental habit of thinking of a Subject in more ways than one, and so presenting even the simplest theme, such as even the two notes of the *first Subject* just quoted, in varied aspects.

The *rhythm* of the opening of this second part (Ex. 201) is also noteworthy; consisting, twice over, of three phrases of two bars, making a six-bar rhythm. The opening of the movement is also worthy your attention, in like manner, for its *un*squareness; the Subject consisting of *ten* bars, instead of the more ordinary *eight*.

Beethoven's Sonata Op. 22 (see Examples 21, 22, 23) has, in that first Movement, very fine presentations of ideas with varied sentiment and character. In the first part this form of passage occurs. (Ex. 202.) The *Codetta* of the

first part opens thus (Ex. 203), the quaver group being an

augmentation of the *Subject figure*, as shown in Ex. 21, here taken as an *inner part*.. After the reiteration of this, the following bold, self-assertive passage occurs. (Ex. 204.) In

(204)

the second part, after some other working, this close imitational presentation of the octave passage occurs (Ex. 205),

(205)

the second bar being the *descending conclusion* of the original passage in Ex. 204, thus brought in, *stretto* fashion, before its time. After much reiteration of this, alternated with working of the Subject figure, and the Arpeggio figure terminating Ex. 202, with modulations, the following is reached (Ex. 206); the Arpeggio figure here being the quiet

accompaniment, and the octave passage appearing as the under part: but how changed! No longer self-assertive and daring, but, in single notes, softly, subordinate, subdued, vanquished! This is continued, in conjunction with a beautiful succession of fundamental discords, till only the last few notes of the subdued passage are reiterated (Ex. 207); and, the conquest being complete, the submission entire, the *ascent*, the *rapprochement*, is made, and then

follows the return to the Subject. Of course this interpretation, æsthetical, if you like to consider it so, is that which it seems to me, individually, to bear; and my work with you is that of *structural analysis*, not poetical or æsthetical interpretation. But this seems to be such a beautiful instance of the æsthetic use of structural skill, that I draw your special attention to it, for your enjoyment: just such a presentation of a musical idea in different aspects as is analogous to the changed aspects of character, in varying circumstances of real life, and under chastening influences.

The first Movement of Beethoven's Sonata Op. 28 (see p. 11) has real double counterpoint, besides other interesting points of working of its beautiful subjects. The first section of ten bars is (Ex. 208).

In the second part these last four bars are, so to speak, detached for separate working, with a double counterpoint drawn from a quaver passage in the first part, leading to the

180   LECTURES ON MUSICAL ANALYSIS.   [LECT.

second Subject. (Ex. 209, 210.) This is taken in G minor

and D minor, and then the last *two* bars are detached and similarly worked. (Ex. 211.) And then, again, *one* bar is so detached and reiterated. (Ex. 212, 213.) In these cases,

observe that the idea is represented in its entirety before being fragmentarily worked, and thus coherence is preserved, and *patchiness* avoided.

Of *Fugal* working, in the second part of a Movement, besides the instance from Beethoven's Op. 111 (Ex. 187, 188), another is furnished by his Sonata Op. 106; the *first Subject* commencing (Ex. 214), being in the second part fugally treated thus. (Ex. 215.)

Imitational devices serve greatly to give life and point,

and prevent flagging or tameness. Imitation in the octave, or, as in Fugue Expositions, in the fifth above or fourth below, are among the most obvious, and are often almost anticipated by an intelligent and moderately experienced listener. But the effect of imitation in unexpected intervals is often indescribably powerful, or *naïve*. We shall see, in considering the conduct of a Fugue, the use made of such less conventional imitations for modulating purposes.

In Mozart's Pianoforte-duet Sonata in F, the *first Subject* of the first *Allegro* begins thus. (Ex. 216.) Again observe the *un*-square rhythm of six bars. The following vigorous

VIII.] MOZART'S DUET IN F. 183

(216) *Allegro di molto.*

passage in the second part is imitationally constructed on the first two bars of the Subject (Ex. 217), the imitation

(217)

1mo.

2ndo.

being firstly in the fifth below, at the distance of two bars, then at the distance of one bar in the octave above, and so on; the music passing through A minor, D minor, G major, C minor, B♭, and to the original Tonic. To the last Movement of this fine Duet I shall refer in another Lecture.

In *concerted* music—for several instruments, that is—there is, obviously, more facility for contrapuntal and imitational interweaving of the parts. In proportion as this characterizes such compositions, they are described as *concertante*. Some *Quartets* for stringed instruments, by Spohr, for instance, are spoken of sometimes as *Solo* Quartets, the meaning being that the first violin is specially prominent, the other instruments doing little more than support it with harmonies. This *show* music may have been very natural for a great violinist like Spohr to write, serving somewhat the purpose of *Chamber Concertos*, so to speak, but lacks the solidity and interest proper to concerted music. Truly, such an opening as this of one of Haydn's Quartets (Ex. 218) is simply a

(218) *Allegro moderato, cantabile.*

VIII.] HAYDN'S QUARTET IN E♭. 185

lovely stream of melody, for the first violin, accompanied by the other instruments. But then, the *prepositional* semi-quaver figure (if the term may be used) is made use of, for the *leggiero* passage immediately following the *cadence*, in the Example; and this and the *Cantabile* Subject are worked in the second part in this wise. (Ex. 219.)

(219)

The return to the Subject is thus effected. (Ex. 220.) Observe the notation here; the B♮ in the first violin having reference to the key *quitted*, C minor; the C♭ in the Viola, to the key *approached*, E♭.

Take, again, the following opening of another Quartet by the same old master. (Ex. 221.) So far it is scarcely more

concertante than that in Example 218. Afterwards, however, the minim theme is taken as the lower part, with florid part superposed; and then, successively, as inner part and lowest part. (Ex. 222.) In the second part it is taken by *inverse movement* as the bass, answered by the first violin. (Ex. 223.) Subsequently it is taken by *diminution*, answered at *cross accent*, with florid accompanying passage (Ex. 224); once more with this close responding. (Ex. 225.) This

188 LECTURES ON MUSICAL ANALYSIS. [LECT.

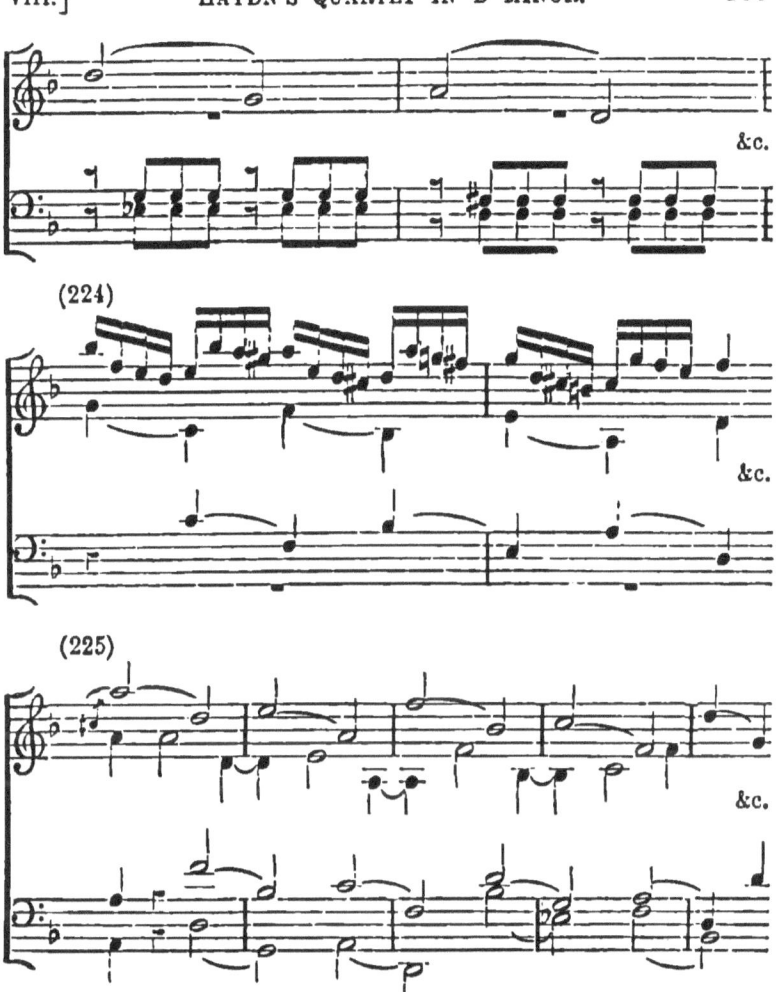

answering at cross accent is, or was, termed imitation *per arsin et thesin;* that which was at the *down* beat being answered at the *up* beat, and *vice versâ*. (See my *Text-book,* § 367.)

Mozart's Quartet No. 2 commences thus (Ex. 226); the effect of the sustained notes in the violoncello, while the inner instruments have repeated notes, being specially

190 LECTURES ON MUSICAL ANALYSIS. [LECT.

(226) *Allegro moderato.*

observable, as is the passing note C in the violoncello, bar 1.

Observe now how this noble theme is imitationally treated in the second part, the entry being a note higher alphabetically, each successive time. (Ex. 227.)

(227)

The last Movement of Mozart's Quartet No. 4 has this *piquant* Subject. (Ex. 228.) In the transitional passage,

leading to the *second Subject*, this phrase occurs. (Ex. 229.) Later on, the concluding two bars of the *first Subject* are taken in the violoncello, with the phrase just quoted, in modified form, for the first violin, and then inverted. (Ex.

(229)

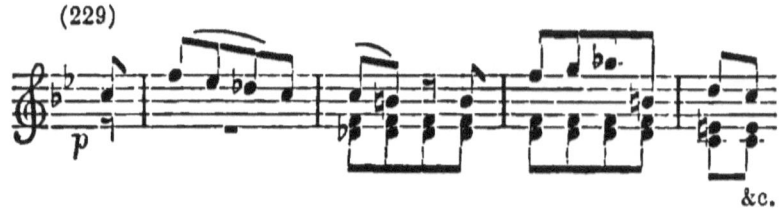

&c.

230.) In the second part this imitational passage, de-

(230)

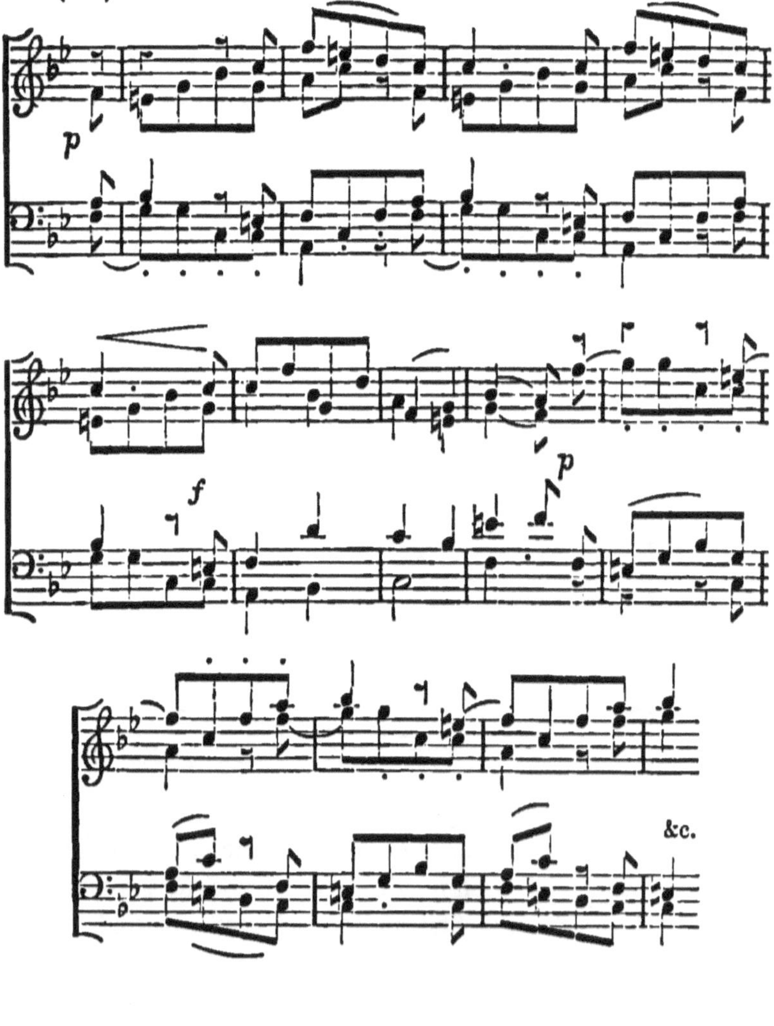

duced from the *first Subject*, occurs. (Ex. 231.) Later on,

new interest is imparted by this Subject being taken on a series of Suspensions, and with the first two notes in augmentation, giving a new rhythmical effect. (Ex. 232.)

The first movement of his Quartet No. 5 has this Subject

of sixteen bars, immediately followed by imitational working successively in the seventh below, the octave below, and the ninth above. (Ex. 233.)

In the second part these additional imitations occur. (Ex. 234, 235.)

Moreover, the third phrase of the Subject commencing at bar 8, is imitationally worked, thus (Ex. 236), and then the last half of it thus (Ex. 237), with changed accent in the imitating part.

(233) *Allegro.*

MOZART'S QUARTET IN A.

MOZART'S QUARTET IN A.

The *second Subject* of this same Movement, so rich in device, commencing in this simple manner (Ex. 238), is

(238)
&c.

immediately afterwards presented imitationally thus. (Ex. 239.)

(239)
&c.

In his Quartet No. 9 the last Movement has a Subject, in itself imitational, commencing thus. (Ex. 240.) Further

(240)

imitations occur in the second part, this extract (Ex. 241) giving the Subject by *inverse* movement in the second violin,

MOZART'S QUARTET NO. 9.

answered successively in the first violin, in the viola by *direct movement*, in the violoncello by *inverse* movement, and so on, at different intervals, above and below, with accompanying thirds and in conjunction with modulation.

Mozart's Quintet No. 3, quoted in Ex. 154, has a *Coda* in which that Subject is thus treated imitationally. (Ex. 242.)

In Beethoven's Quintet, Op. 29, the Subject quoted in Ex. 46 is thus worked imitationally in the second part (Ex. 243), started by the second viola, answered a fifth above by the first viola, then a fifth above that by the second violin, and a fifth above that by the first violin.

In all such chamber-music, one charm is the integrity of clear part-writing, without any adventitious or meretricious effects, to conceal any paucity of material. A Quartet should

neither be *orchestral* in its aim and character, nor a *Solo* with accompaniment, but should be, to coin a term, quartet-ish, with legitimate *concertante* structure and effects. And, in listening to music, it is important for you in criticizing it, which means bringing it to *judgment* (for the intelligent increase of your enjoyment, not for captiousness), to bear in mind what it *purports* to be; what resources, vocal or instrumental, are available, and what the proper limits of its legitimate effects.

In Beethoven's well-known Septet Op. 20, for Clarionet, Bassoon, Horn, Violin, Viola, Violoncello, and Double-bass, the last Movement begins thus. (Ex. 244.) In the second

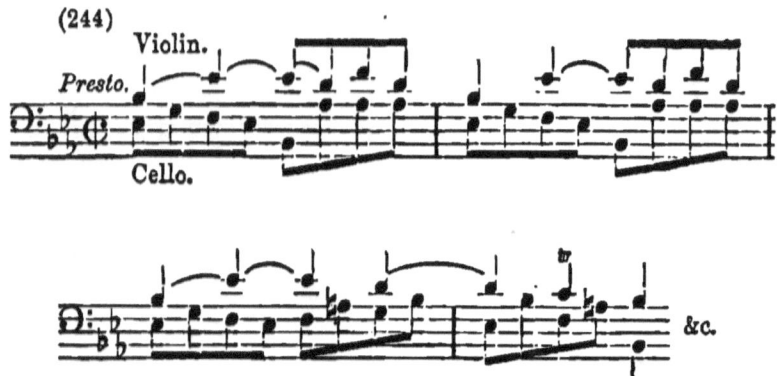

part this theme is closely worked thus. (Ex. 245.) Such works as this, and Spohr's *Nonet* for stringed and wind instruments combined, seem midway between Chamber-music and Orchestral; having the opportunity for the con-

trasts of tone which assist to give *colouring*, as it is termed, a term borrowed from another art; while having, at the same time, the delicacy which comes from single instruments, no doubling of the stringed instruments, and no instruments of percussion.

It has been impossible, had it been desirable, in this survey of some of the methods of working Subjects and developing ideas, to separate them from one another. Imitation, inversion of parts, inverse movement, rhythmical devices, together with modulation and changed harmonies, interlace one another, and combine in various, indeed multifarious, manners, to expound subjects, and produce coherence, continuity, interdependence, and all this with unstudied ease. I have sought by these specimens and comments to direct your thoughts, so that you may know how to do the same sort of thing for yourselves.

I have just used the term "unstudied ease." For remember, again, that the perfection of art is to conceal art; or, as Mr. Swinburne puts it, in one of his *Roundels*, entitled '*A Singing Lesson*'—

"FAR-FETCHED and dear-bought, as the proverb rehearses,
  Is good, or was held so, for ladies : but nought
  In a song can be good if the turn of the verse is
    Far-fetched and dear-bought.

"As the turn of a wave should it sound, and the thought
Ring smooth, and as light as the spray that disperses
Be the gleam of the words for the garb thereof wrought.

"Let the soul in it shine through the sound as it pierces
Men's hearts with possession of music unsought;
For the bounties of song are no jealous god's mercies,
Far-fetched and dear-bought." *

---

* *A Century of Roundels*, lxvii.

LECTURE IX.

MOVEMENT OF EPISODE. MUCH WITH REGARD TO IT IN COMMON WITH MOVEMENT OF CONTINUITY. EPISODE DEFINED. SOMETIMES BEARS ON THE REST OF THE MOVEMENT. INSTANCES FROM BEETHOVEN'S OP. 14 AND OP. 2. MOVEMENT OF DEVELOPMENT MAY HAVE EPISODICAL MATTER. EPISODICAL MOVEMENT MAY HAVE DEVELOPMENT. MOVEMENT WITH ONE EPISODE. EXAMPLES FROM HAYDN, MOZART, AND BEETHOVEN. RONDO: ANALOGOUS TERMS. SOME RONDOS, NOT SO TERMED. SOME MOVEMENTS, MISNAMED RONDOS. CONCISE EXAMPLES FROM COUPERIN AND RAMEAU. EXAMPLE FROM BACH'S SECOND PARTITA.

IX.

WE will now consider another kind of Movement than that which has hitherto engaged our attention: the EPISODICAL, as distinguished from the *first-movement*, or *Sonata* form, or plan. Very much of that which I have already told you, and illustrated to you from so many fine works, applies to this different kind of Movement as well as to the Movement of continuity: in fact, applies to all structures. Subjects, Rhythm, Harmony, Melody, Counterpoint, Imitation, these enter, in various degrees, into structural music generally; and therefore it has not been a disproportionate amount of time and attention that we have ostensibly given to the one structure, seeing that the structure in question is so comprehensive and inclusive, and the consideration of it at so great a length has anticipated and prepared the way for much else, and will render unnecessary so much detailed and technical explanation with regard to works of another plan. But, after all, Musical Composition is so boundless a subject to deal with, in extent and in interest, that no number of Lectures would exhaust it.

An EPISODE, as I have previously told you (Lecture VI.), is, analogously with its meaning in other cases,—history, fiction, and the like,—a Subject or passage not connected with the main current of the Movement, but introduced by way of contrast or relief: sometimes, moreover, made to have a bearing upon the rest of the Movement. Thus, in the first Movement of Beethoven's Sonata Op. 14, No. 1 (see Ex. 13, &c., and Ex. 131, in Lect. VI.), the *Episode* in the second part seems like a somewhat stormy interruption to the placid flow of the Movement; or, shall we say, an impassioned outburst, interrupting the exquisite interchange of affection which characterizes all the rest, rendering most delightful the calm, though somewhat more joyous, resumption of the original *Subject*. But there is no *working* of that *Episode*: it is purely episodical.

On the other hand the last Movement of Beethoven's Sonata Op. 2, No. 1 (on the first Movement of which I have said so much in the third, fourth, and sixth Lectures), is a Movement of continuity, but has an *Episode* of great length in the second part. The first part, marked by great fire and motion, terminates in C minor, the *Subject* having been in F minor. Then the second part opens with the lovely stream of continuous melody commencing (Ex. 246),

as though trying by tender entreaty to obtain that which feverish excitement and active persistency, almost obstinacy, had failed to win. But the activity is then resumed, and continued to the end.

The *first* Movement of Mozart's Quartet No. 4 (of which the last Movement is referred to in Lecture VIII.) has a charming *Episode*, opening the second part; but it is not worked in the after-part of the Movement.

Such *Episodes* as these, then, do not constitute the Movements in which they occur *Episodical*: they remain Movements of *Continuity* or *Development*. A life marked by singleness of earnest purpose may have its interruptions, pleasurable or otherwise, intentional or inevitable; its pauses for reflection, its seasons of relaxation; but these do not render the life *fitful*, a mere series of unconnected incidents.

On the other hand, an *Episodical* Movement may, as we shall see, have some working, or development, bringing together of *Subjects*, and so forth; but that will not alter the fact of its being a Movement of *Episode*, rather than of *continuity*, or so-called *Sonata form*.

In its simplest form, a Movement of the kind that we are beginning to consider consists of a *Subject* in one key, more or less complete in itself; then another *Subject*, the EPISODE, in a related key, again more or less complete in itself; and then a return to the original *Subject* and key, with, perhaps, a *Coda* or *Codetta*. I have used the expression "more or less complete in itself," of these two *Subjects*, because either or both of them may *close* in their respective keys, being thereby rendered complete; or they may lead into one another. If both *Subject* and *Episode* close in their respective keys, the *Episode* becomes, in fact, a *Movement within a Movement*; especially if there be no connecting passages, either from *Subject* to *Episode*, or for the return.

This kind of Movement, with *one Episode*, is about the simplest and easiest to construct that is possible; requiring no developing or *sustained* power, no rhythmical devices, but only good melody, good harmony (well laid out), regular rhythm, and sense of proportion, fitness, and congruity. Moreover, it is easy to follow, and does not tax the attention; being therefore an acceptable relief, in a Sonata, Symphony, or the like, after a Movement of larger proportions, which has required tension of mind to listen to. And it is the structure adopted for a great proportion of single, fugitive, light (not by any means meaning *bad*) pieces, such as *Nocturnes, Valses de Salon*, &c. A *Minuet* and *Trio*, with *Da Capo*, is *Episodical*, taken as a whole; though I shall

P

have more to say about this in another Lecture. And many *slow Movements* of Sonatas, &c. are of this plan.

Haydn's Sonata No. 32, the first Movement of which is quoted in Examples 28, 29, and 197, has a slow Movement in B♭ Major, commencing (Ex. 247). This modulates to F,

returns to B♭, and closes in that key: after which, this *Episode*, in the *Tonic Minor*, commences (Ex. 248), modu-

lates to D♭,—a great relief, this change of Tonic,—has a repeat and a second part, but not a return to its own *Subject*. A *half-close* is made upon the Dominant, and then the original *first Subject* in B♭ major recurs, and, with embellishments and a *Coda*, the Movement is concluded.

His Sonata No. 34, quoted in Examples 145 to 148, has a slow Movement in E major, commencing (Ex. 249). This

(249) *Adagio.*

portion of the Movement has its modulation to the Dominant repeat, second part, return to, and close in the key. Then follows this *Episode* (Ex. 250) in the *Tonic Minor*, which

(250)

modulates to G major, returns to E minor, but, like the last-mentioned Movement, proceeds to a half-close, and so leads back to the original Subject.

Mozart's Sonata No. 10 (see Example 130) has a slow Movement in F major (Ex. 251), with its own modulation to

(251) *Andante cantabile.*

the Dominant, &c., and close in the key. This *Episode* in F minor (Ex. 252) also is complete in itself, and closes in

its own key and mode. To this are affixed four bars, serving as *Intermezzo*,—*i. e.* put in between,—not, however, leading back to the *first Subject*, but closing again, like a *Codetta*, in F minor. Then the original first portion of the Movement is recapitulated, and the *Intermezzo* is changed, and, so to speak, translated into F *major*, to serve as a Codetta to the whole Movement.

The slow Movement of his Sonata No. 14 (for first Movement see Examples 55 to 58, 90, 91) is also Episodical. The first portion is in E♭ (Ex. 253), with second part in the

key of the Dominant, returning to, and closing in the original key. The *Episode* (Ex. 254) is in the *Sub-dominant*, A♭, with second part in G♭, from which it passes, through

C minor, to a half-close on the Dominant of the original key, and, with modifications, the first portion is recapitulated.

His Sonata No. 19, from the first Movement of which I have quoted somewhat copiously in my *Text-book*, pp. 178, 179, has an Episodical slow Movement in A (Ex. 255), the

Episode being in F♯ minor, and of considerable extent.

(Ex. 256.) The figure of this *Episode* is used, in A major,

for the *Codetta* to the Movement. The *Episode* closes in its own key, but there is an intermediate passage of a few bars to lead back to the *first Subject*.

Beethoven's Sonatas Op. 13, Op. 28, and Op. 79 have slow Movements of this simple Episodical structure.

The slow Movement of the '*Pathétique*,' Op. 13, has this *Subject* (Ex. 257), which, with its own second part (Ex.

258), passing through F minor and E♭, then closes in its own

key. Then comes this *Episode* in the *Tonic Minor* (Ex. 259), specially beautiful in the contrasted characters of the

(259)

extreme parts, which does not close in the key, but, by a modulating passage, leads back to the *first Subject*, with Triplet accompaniment, to which is appended a *Codetta*. Notice, however, the wonderfully bright modulation in this *Episode*, which may appear to be *enharmonic;* whereas the *notation* only is so, *not* the *modulation*. (Ex. 260.) Had

(260)

216   LECTURES ON MUSICAL ANALYSIS.   [LECT.

the first bar of Example been written as the harmony of G♯ minor, instead of A♭ minor, the connection with that which follows it would have been obvious; and, also obviously, this would only have been enharmonic change of *notation* with reference to that which *precedes* it. Had there been no change of notation, the modulation would have been to the inconvenient key of F♭ *minor!* (See my *Text-book*, p. 167.) The slow Movement of the (so-called) *Pastoral* Sonata, Op. 28, has a complete *Subject*, with first and second parts (Ex. 261); and a charmingly contrasted *Episode* (Ex. 262), also

quite complete, terminating in its own *Major Mode*. The *Subject*, on its recapitulation, is greatly embellished. The *Coda* of the Movement is compounded, fragmentarily, of both *Subjects*.

The *Subject* and *Episode* of the slow Movement of the Sonata Op. 79 commence, respectively, thus (Ex. 263, 264); and there is a *Codetta* of (through broken rhythm) the irregular number of *five* bars.

IX.] SIMPLE EPISODICAL MOVEMENTS. 217

(263) *Andante.*

&c.

(264)

&c.

Now in all these cases the *Subject* is complete in itself, closes in its own key, and might be a little Movement by itself. And in some of them—Mozart, No. 10, and Beethoven, Op. 28 and Op. 79—the *Episode* is likewise complete in itself, with its own close. In the other cases, the *Episode* does not so close, but, by *half-close* or otherwise, leads back to the *first Subject*. There is, however, only *one Episode;* except perhaps the No. 14 of Mozart, which *may* be reckoned as having *two*, that which I have reckoned as the second part of the *first Subject* being considered as an *Episode*. And similarly, in Beethoven's Op. 13, the phrase beginning at Example 258 might by some be reckoned as *first Episode*, instead of second part of *first Subject*. Waiving these two cases, however, the Examples thus far adduced are of *simple Episodical Movements*, without development: the *Episodes* not reappearing, except in those cases in which there is a reminiscence as *Codetta*.

Those who term the *Sonata* form the *Binary* or *Duplex*

form, term this *Episodical* form the *Trinary* or *Triplex* form.

When, however, there is more than one *Episode*, and therefore at least two *returns* to the *Subject*, the *Episodical Movement* is termed a *Rondo* (Fr. *Rondeau*)—the word meaning *round*, and designating the *coming round* to the *Subject*. The term *Round*, however, is applied to a particular kind of *Vocal Canon*, and we do not use the English word to designate the *Episodical* Movement that we are now considering. Analogous words, such as *Rondel, Roundel, Roundelay*, used to designate certain forms of verse or song, with or without music, seem to refer to the same point in structure—the coming *round* to an original phrase. Also, probably, to some *round dances*, or songs with dance. Waiving, however, these terms and their uses, though I shall myself "*come round*" to one of them presently, I have to direct your attention to the *Rondo* as commonly understood by musicians. The *diminutives* of this word are *Rondino* and *Rondoletto*, either term being applied to a Movement of this structure, when the Subjects, *first Subject* and *Episodes*, are short, rather than to a *simple Episodical* Movement such as those that I have already referred to. We are considering *instrumental* music; but there are *Vocal Rondos: e.g.* one by Mozart, with pianoforte accompaniment,—"*Non temer amato bene;*" one in an opera by Sir. G. A. Macfarren, &c.

I will premise two things. First of all, that many *Rondos* are not so called; that is, the title is not prefixed. For instance, the two *Polonaises* or *Polaccas*, by Weber, are in *Rondo* form, but this is not specified in the title. Sterndale Bennett's *Rondeau à la Polonaise* expresses in its title at once the *character* and the *structure* of the Movement. The *Rondo form* may be allied either with a *dance-measure* or with any other characteristic style. A notion prevails popularly, and has even been expressed in printed definitions, that a *Rondo* is a cheerful, even light composition. This is quite a mistake; the word simply designates *structure*, not *character*. We shall have illustrations of this.

The second matter that I premise is that some compositions are termed *Rondos* which are not in *Rondo form*. A Movement of continuity by Mozart, of the clearest structure, commencing (Ex. 265), is entitled *Rondo in D*. Likewise a

posthumous Movement in B♭ by him, commencing (Ex. 266),

is entitled a *Rondo*. Both of these are misnamed *Rondos*. Other instances will come before us. While on this subject, however, I may as well so far anticipate as to say, that, just as some first Movements, as we have seen, have *Episodical matter* in them, but still remain Movements of *development*, so, on the other hand, as we shall see, a *Rondo* may have some *development* in it, and still be an *Episodical Movement;* such development taking the place of an *Episode*.

Among the earliest *Rondeaux*, expressly and rightly so styled, are some in the *Suites* by François Couperin, *le grand*, as he is called,—1668-1733,—Court Clavicordist to Louis XIV., and organist to the Royal Chapel. He gave very fanciful titles to his pieces, the interpretation of which is not very plain to us; said, however, to have had reference to persons or events which had been suggestive to the composer. A *Rondo* entitled *Sœur Monique* has a *Subject* in F of eight bars, commencing (Ex. 267), which is repeated; then an

Episode of six bars, commencing and ending in C (Ex. 268),

which might be considered a second part of the *Subject*, to which it then returns. Then follows an *Episode* of fourteen bars, commencing (Ex. 269) in G minor, passing through D

minor, and then leading through C to the *Subject* in the original key. There is no change of accent or character thus far; but then comes an *Episode* (Ex. 270) in the key of the

Movement, with semiquaver accompaniment, which, moreover, ends in F—an unusual structure—prior to the final resumption of the *Subject*, with which this little *Rondeau* terminates.

Other *Rondeaux* by Couperin are entitled *Les Sylvains, Les Abeilles, L'Enchanteresse, La Badine, La Bandoline, Le Dodo, ou L'Amour au Berceau*, which last double title may interest some of you little girls. It begins (Ex. 271); but we are accustomed to have a *Berceuse* in ⁶⁄₈ time. I suppose,

however, that you can sing your doll to sleep in *simple* time as well as in *compound*.

Another example of about the same period is by Jean Phillipe Rameau, 1683—1764, eminent as clavicordist, organist, composer, and theorist. (See p. 22.) This is a *Tambourin*, a dance accompanied by the instrument so named. It is entirely on a *Tonic Pedal-bass*, and does not quit the key of E minor. The *Subject* begins (Ex. 272, *a*),

the *three Episodes* begin (*b, c, d*), and lead into the *Subject* in each case; that *Subject* being varied in the final instance.

These very simple and concise specimens may prepare you for the more elaborate compositions of later times which we shall consider. The characteristics of these by Couperin and Rameau are continuousness and congruity, rather than contrast of accent or even of key.

In advance of these, in contrapuntal working, is the *Rondeau* (not the final Movement) from Bach's *Partita* No. 2, commencing (Ex. 273), the *Subject* itself being

slightly imitational. The first *Episode* (or second part of the *Subject*) commences in E♭ (Ex. 274), and works through

F minor to a half-close in C minor, re-introducing the *Subject*, with counterpoint to the first bar. The next *Episode*, of sixteen bars, commences (Ex. 275) in C minor,

(275)

and passes through E♭, leading to a *Variation* of the *Subject* (Ex. 276), an excellent device in a *Rondo*. The next *Episode*

(276)

is principally in G minor, commencing (Ex. 277). At the

(277)

ninth bar of this *Episode* a most notable device is employed: the original *Subject* is taken as the bass, with a semiquaver counterpoint superposed (Ex. 278) and, imitationally, the

RONDO FROM BACH'S SECOND PARTITA.

(278)

Subject, again varied, is returned to in the original key, and with this the Movement closes. With the exception of the opening of the last *Episode*, it is in only two parts; but the contrapuntal integrity of those parts prevents any thought of thinness or poverty. Any attempt to "enrich" it by modern filling up would interfere with its beautiful clearness. Those who perpetrate such additions or alterations manifest their own poverty of apprehension as to the integral worth of a work of art, and are guilty of an anachronism in art.

LECTURE X.

RONDO, *continued:* SHOULD BE CONTINUOUS. FINAL MOVEMENTS OF SONATAS, ETC., OFTEN IN THIS FORM. EXAMPLES FROM HAYDN'S SONATAS AND QUARTETS; MOZART'S SONATAS, RONDO IN A MINOR, AND DUET IN F.

X.

THE word *Rondo* meaning *round*, and being applied to a Movement in which there is more than one *coming round* to the *Subject*, it seems to follow that, though an *Episode* is defined as a Movement within a Movement, having no direct bearing on or connection with that which precedes and follows it, yet in a true *Rondo* the *Subject* should not merely *succeed* an interposed *Episode*, but should be *come round* to in continuity. Therefore, in my opinion, the intermediate matter, between the appearances of the *first Subject*, is not, in a true *Rondo*, Episodical, in the sense above given; and should not be detached from it, or at both ends: it should be part of the *circle*, the *round*. There may, indeed, be just such a momentary cadence as, in a round dance, might be required for breath-taking; or as occurs at the end of each *stanza* in a continuous little poem; but it should not fail to *go on:* there should be, so to speak, *circular impulse*, if the expression may be used. This condition is fulfilled in the *Rondos* by Couperin, Rameau, and Bach, already quoted; but seems to be lost sight of in many so-called *Rondos*.

In the Sonatas of Hadyn, Mozart, Dussek, Clementi, Beethoven, and many modern writers, the *Rondo* form is frequently adopted for the last Movement. The only one of Haydn's which is so entitled is the last Movement of No. 24, commencing with a *Subject* of six-bar rhythm. (Ex. 279.) After this has definitely closed in the key, a transitional

(279) *Presto.*

passage is introduced, according to the manner of a first Movement, leading to a *second Subject* in the key of the Dominant, very much in the style of the *first Subject.* Then a few bars lead back to the *first Subject,* and this is followed by an *Episode* in C minor, commencing (Ex. 280), modulat-

(280)

ing to E♭, referring to some passages in the *first Subject,* introducing an imitational passage on one figure from it (Ex. 281), and working to a half-close in the original key, in

(281)

which the *first Subject* then returns, followed by some of the transitional matter previously referred to, the *second Subject*, still in C, and a *Coda*. So that the Movement has more of the structure of a first Movement than its title would indicate.

The *Finale* of No. 20 is in *Rondo* form. The *Subject* commences (Ex. 282); the *first Episode* is in D minor, with

(282) *Allegro assai.*

&c.

modulation to F. (Ex. 283.) The *first Subject* then re-

(283)

L. H. in 8ves.

appears, varied thus (Ex. 284). A *second Episode* appears

(284)

&c.

in A (Ex. 285), followed by another variation of the *first*

(285)

&c.

232   LECTURES ON MUSICAL ANALYSIS.   [LECT.

Subject (Ex. 286), and then a *Coda*. The *Subject* in all

three cases, and both *Episodes*, close in their respective keys, and there is no connecting matter; but there is *Rondo impulse* about it.

The same remarks apply to the *Finale* of No. 30, the *first Movement* of which is quoted in Example 1, page 6. In this last Movement, however, though the *Subject* and *Episodes* are self-contained, there is an *intermezzo* passage after the *second Episode*.

The *Finales* of Nos. 5 (for *first Movement* see Ex. 24), 6, and 10 have been published separately as *Rondos;* but they are of *development* structure. Their respective *first Subjects* are Examples 287, 288, 289.

The *first Movement* of Nos. 6, 12, 19 (also the *Finale*), and 24, are in *Episodical* form.

(289) *Presto.* No. 10.

The *Finale* of Haydn's *String* Quartet in C, commencing (Ex. 290), is expressly termed a *Rondo*. The *Episode* is in

(290) *Presto.*

A minor (Ex. 291), and, after the return to the *Subject*, recurs in C minor, the *Subject* being worked in with it, in continuity.

(291)

The *Finale* of another of his Quartets, in D, though not termed a *Rondo*, is quite a "merry-go-round" for unceasing activity and jollity. Commencing with this *Subject* (Ex. 292), there is only one bar's cessation of semiquaver motion till the few chords preceding the final cadence; so you may know that Weber was not the first to write a "*moto continuo.*" But the principal *Episode* in D minor is worthy of

your special attention: the semiquaver Movement, in unbroken continuity from the preceding portion, forming a counterpoint to a new theme; and the working, with inversion of *Subject* and *Counterpoint*, being fugal. (Ex. 293.)

We get *continuity*, and sometimes more *development*, as we advance to the *Rondos* of Mozart's Sonatas. That of No. 3, in B♭, commencing (Ex. 294), has, after the close of the

(294) *Allegro.*

Subject, a transitional passage, leading to a *second Subject* (or *first Episode*) in the Dominant (Ex. 295), and then the

(295)

return to the *first Subject*. An *Episode* in G minor, in two Sections (Ex. 296), follows, with *Cadence* in that key: a

(296)

connecting three bars leads to a resumption of the *Subject.* Then another *Episode* in E♭ (Ex. 297), passing through C

minor, leads to a *half-close* in the original key, and the *Subject*, with the transitional matter, and *second Subject* (Ex. 295), still in the key; and then one more recurrence of the *Subject* terminates the Movement. This is similar in structure to that of Haydn's No. 24; and it seems, perhaps, more natural to regard that which I have designated the *second Subject* as a *second part* of the *first Subject;* in this case of Mozart's, at all events: in both cases it may be said that there is, so to speak, a complete little Movement *in the original key*, with transient, tributary modulation, prior to the occurrence of any *Episode*, properly so called.

Similarly with the *Rondo* of his Sonata No. 7, the first Movement of which is referred to at page 19. The *Rondo* commences (Ex. 298), and then proceeds like a first Movement,

with *second Subject* (Ex. 299) and *Codetta* (Ex. 300). Then instead of the expected repeat, as in a first Movement, the *first Subject* recurs followed by an *Episode* in F (Ex. 301),

X.] MOZART'S RONDOS. 237

modulating to D minor, thence to C, the original key; not to the *first Subject*, however, but to some of the matter which, in the first part, had appeared in the Dominant. After this the *Subject* re-enters, and there is no further modulation; a neat little *Codetta*, founded on the *Subject*, terminating the Movement.

The *Rondo* of No. 9, the first Movement of which is quoted, Examples 135, 136, 137, is of a similar structure. So is that of No. 13, in B♭, which is noteworthy for a *Cadenza*, following a pause on a $\frac{6}{4}$, after the manner of a Concerto. The *Rondo* of his Sonata No. 20, in B♭, the first Movement of which I have analyzed in my *Text-book*, page 211 *et seq.*, is of similar plan, but is mainly noticeable for its extraneous modulations. After the *second Subject* in F, and the return to the *first Subject*, an *Episode* in E♭ appears, from which a modulation to B♮ major is effected, by the series of harmonies represented by this figured bass. (Ex. 302.) In this remote key the *first Subject* is taken, and then

modulation is effected through B minor to G major, in which the *Subject* again appears, and shortly afterwards, by this course of harmonies (Ex. 303), return is made to the original key.

The Sonata No. 11, in A, has not one Movement in Sonata form. It opens with an air with variations, is followed by a Minuet and Trio, in A and D respectively, and the *Finale* is the famous *Rondo alla Turca*, in A minor and major, in which, however, there is only *one Episode*, though that is of *four Sections*. After the repetition of the *Subject*, one section of that *Episode* is repeated in slightly changed form, and then a *Coda* terminates the Movement.

The *middle Movement* of his Sonata No. 6 is a *Rondeau en Polonaise*, with, however, only *one Episode*.

The *Finale* of his Sonata No. 8, on the *first Movement* of which I have commented in connection with Examples 53, 54, 88, 89, 141, is a vigorous *Rondo* (Ex. 304), the first part

of which modulates through C to E minor, in which a modification of the *Subject* is taken as the bass for a *second Subject* (Ex. 305), after which return is made to the original

key and *Subject*. Then follows an *Episode* in the *Tonic major* (Ex. 306); and a recapitulation of the first part, with modification to keep in the key, and a *Coda*, conclude the Movement. Thus some features of *first Movement plan* are here, as in some of the previous instances, associated with *Rondo form*.

This is also the case with the magnificent *Finale* of the Sonata No. 14. I have commented on the first Movement,

240 LECTURES ON MUSICAL ANALYSIS. [LECT.

(306)

in connection with Examples 55 to 58, 90, 91, 143; and on the slow Movement, in this Lecture. This *Finale* has a three-fold *Subject*. (Examples 307, 308, 309.) At the con-

(307) *Allegro assai.*

(308)

Bis

(309)

clusion of this, one Dominant chord leads at once to E♭, in which is the *second Subject*, which may be termed twofold. (Examples 310, 311.) The original *Subject* then recurs,

(310)

(311)

after a few bars of modulation; and then, instead of a close in C minor, two bars lead to F minor, in which this *Episode* is given (Ex. 312), and reiterated in G minor. Then, the

(312)

second Subject (Ex. 310) is taken in C minor, followed by the *first Subject*, which is interrupted by a passage *a piacere* (at pleasure), being somewhat of the nature of a *Recitative*, a passage of soliloquy. The *first Subject* is then resumed, and, with matter from the first part, and a *Coda*, the Movement finishes. There is nothing in it of the

R

disjointedness which sometimes marks a *Rondo*, although there are many rests and pauses, which are of great power.

The *Rondo* of the Sonata No. 15, on the first Movement of which I have made many remarks in Lecture VII., is specially to be noticed for the *contrast* between the various *Subjects*. The sweet simplicity of the *first Subject* (Ex. 313) is quite childlike, without any puerility however. It

is of considerable length, with modulation to the Dominant, and recurrence to the original key. Just as it closes, and one is beginning to ask, "Is it all to be so simple?" this bold *Episode* in D minor (Ex. 314) suddenly breaks in. At its

close is a quiet appendix in B♭ (Ex. 315), followed by a return to the *Subject*, which is given briefly. Then follows

(315)

this smooth, imitational *Episode* in F minor (Ex. 316),

modulating to A♭, with a second part modulating through B♮ minor, and returning to the *Subject* of this *Episode* in the bass, the imitational parts being inverted. (Ex. 317.)

The original *Subject* is soon resumed, and some of the first part recapitulated. Then comes the *Coda*, commencing with this fine piling up of the parts, with the *figure*, though not the precise intervals, of the *Subject*. (Ex. 318.) Towards the close, the *Subject*, with modification, has a *Counterpoint* added (Ex. 319), and a few bars close this Movement of such varied interest, unity, and contrast.

(318)

(319)

I have commented on the Episodical slow Movement of No. 19. The *Finale* is in *Rondo* form; the Episodical portion following the first recurrence of the *Subject* being, however, somewhat of the nature of development, passing through several keys. Such a Movement as this may almost be said to be like a *first Movement*, with the repetition of the *Subject* interpolated between the first and second parts. I must not pass over this Movement, however, without calling your attention to the way in which the *first Subject* (Ex. 320) is made the basis of the *second Subject* (Ex. 321), and

(320) *Allegretto.*

(321)

then worked by inverse imitation, thus (Ex. 322), and in the second part by direct imitation. (Ex. 323.)

One of the most perfect even of Mozart's perfect works is

the *Rondo* in A minor: music not for show or sensation, but for thoughtful enjoyment in your own quiet room. It opens with a remarkable *Subject* on a *Tonic-pedal* (Ex. 324)

which, after a close at the eighth bar, has its own second part in C (Ex. 325), returning to the first phrase, and ending in the original key: it is complete in itself.

Then follows an *Episode* in F (Ex. 326), of a singing character, and in excellent contrast to the *Subject*. This modulates to and closes its first part in C; and then the second part passes through G minor, F minor, D♭, and

248 LECTURES ON MUSICAL ANALYSIS. [LECT.

returns to F major, in which there is a close, immediately succeeded by a long connecting passage, leading back to the original *first Subject*, of which only the first eight bars are taken.

The next *Episode* is in the *Tonic major* (Ex. 327), with

modulation to the Dominant, second part, and return to its own theme, closing in the key; and then, as after the *first Episode*, a long connecting passage, leading back again to the *first Subject*: this *connecting* passage, moreover, being also, paradoxical as it might seem, a *dissociating* passage, to change the current of thought from the *Tonic A* and its immediate surroundings: the return to it, in the minor mode, being then a true *return home*. After the *Subject* has been repeated, with embellishment, and some little appended matter, a most remarkable *Coda* follows. The *Subject* enters at the different half of the bar from that in which it first appeared, and in the middle of a contrapuntal passage, giving changed harmonies to the *Subject*. (Ex. 328.) The *Subject*

(328)

is then taken as the bass of a similar, not identical passage. (Ex. 329.) A reminiscence of the *second Episode* follows,

(329)

leading to a *Tonic pedal*, on which a final reference to the *Subject* is made (Ex. 330) and the noble Movement closes. An unvitiated taste must be brought to such music as this, to appreciate and enjoy it.

There is also a *Rondo* in F by Mozart, originally composed for a musical-box, or clock, which is quite worthy your analysis.

I referred, in Lecture VIII., p. 182, to Mozart's Pianoforte Duet Sonata in F. The final *Rondo* (not so termed) is of great power. The *Subject* is of remarkable rhythm: two phrases of five bars each. (Ex. 331.) At the return, this is

prolonged imitationally, thus (Ex. 332); and, later on, thus (Ex. 333).

LECTURE XI.

RONDO FORM, *continued*. GRADUAL EXTENSION OF THE RONDO, FROM COUPERIN AND RAMEAU, BACH, HAYDN, MOZART. PARTIAL ADOPTION OF FIRST MOVEMENT FORM IN CONJUNCTION WITH RONDO STRUCTURE. INSTANCES IN BEETHOVEN'S SONATAS. THE IDEAL OF A RONDO: ROUNDNESS. ILLUSTRATION AND DEFINITION IN ROUNDEL BY MR. SWINBURNE. EXAMPLE FROM DUSSEK'S OP. 35. DUSSEK CHARACTERIZED. RONDOS BY BEETHOVEN: OP. 7; OP. 2, NO. 2; OP. 28; OP. 31, NO. 1; OP. 51, NO. 2. REMARKS ABOUT RONDOS BY WEBER, HERZ, MENDELSSOHN, BENNETT: SOME OF THEM NOT JUSTIFYING THEIR TITLES. EPISODICAL MOVEMENT BY THE LECTURER REFERRED TO. GENERAL REQUIREMENTS IN STRUCTURE.

XI.

IN the *Rondos* which we first of all examined, the *episodical* portions hardly assumed the character of fresh *Subjects:* they were rather continuations of the *Subject*, with its general character and accent. In Bach (Examples 273—278) there was some advance upon this structure: more change, both of key and accent, but still, continuity. In some of Haydn's *Rondos*, the *Episodes* are still more distinctly detached, by *cadences;* but in others the continuity is maintained, and the first part is of first Movement form; the second *Episode* being somewhat of the nature of development. This structure, again, we saw further exemplified in some of Mozart's *Rondos;* though in others, both by Haydn and Mozart, the *second Episode* is *purely episodical*, being new material.

This *first movement* structure for the first part of a *Rondo* is adopted by Beethoven in several of his Sonata *Finales: e. g.* Op. 2, No. 3, Op. 13, Op. 31, No. 1. That is to say, there is transitional, connecting matter, leading in continuity from the *first Subject* to the *second*, which *second Subject*, therefore, is not *episodical*. But, whether *second Subject*, in continuity, or *episodical Subject*, or *Episode of development*, they all come *round* to the *first Subject*. So that the first complete idea in a *Rondo* is both *Subject* and *Refrain*, starting-point and goal : I might almost say, *Nominative* and *Accusative*. At least this seems to me the *ideal* of a *Rondo:* the *Subject* holding an analogous position to the words " Farfetched and dear-bought," in the *Roundel* " A Singing Lesson," which I made free to quote at the end of Lecture VIII. Or, if possible, even more appositely, according to the beautifully combined definition and example furnished by the *Roundel* LXIII. of the same series:

> "A ROUNDEL is wrought as a ring or a starbright sphere,
> With craft of delight and with cunning of sound unsought,
> That the heart of the hearer may smile if to pleasure his ear
>   A roundel is wrought.
>
> Its jewel of music is carven of all or of aught—
> Love, laughter, or mourning, remembrance of rapture or fear—
> That fancy may fashion to hang in the ear of thought.
>
> As a bird's quick song runs round, and the hearts in us hear
> Pause answer to pause, and again the same strain caught,
> So moves the device whence, round as a pearl or a tear,
>   A roundel is wrought."

This exquisite instance of a definition being itself the thing defined may indeed indicate the nature of spontaneous music of any kind; but it is specially applicable to a genuine *Rondo*, which should be "wrought as a ring," in which is no break to the roundness: it needs "craft"—workmanship—"of delight," "that the heart of the hearer may smile;" there being a peculiar "pleasure" in the return to the *Subject*, if effected with *naïveté*, with "cunning of sound unsought." However much "pause" may "answer to pause" at each *Episode*, yet if there be "again the same strain caught," "round as a pearl or a tear," so a "*Rondo* is wrought." But there needs, for this finished roundness, not only skill in working round, but a certain adaptability in the *Subject* itself, to be either moving, starting impulse, or result; like the phrase "a roundel is wrought."

A very happy example of this is furnished by the *Rondo* of Dussek's Sonata Op. 35, No. 2, of which the melodious *Subject* (Ex. 334), commencing with the Dominant 7th, makes, in its first phrase, a beautifully satisfactory termination, wherever it recurs after *episodical* matter.

(334) *Molto Allegro con Espressione.*

In a greater or less degree, the same characteristic is to be noted in other *Rondos* by Dussek: such as that to the "*Farewell*" Sonata, previously alluded to (Lecture V.), the "*Elegy*" Sonata, "*L'Invocation*" Sonata, and others. The well-known piece by him entitled "*La Consolation*" is in *episodical* form, but the two *Episodes* in the *Tonic minor* and the *Sub-dominant major* do not lead into or *round* to the *Subject*, being complete in themselves, with their own *cadences*: the *second Episode*, however, having an appendix, with a transitional passage, to modulate back to the original key. Some editions of this piece are provokingly without its beautiful *Introduction*. A Movement of somewhat similar construction, and of varied interest and beauty, is the *Andante* in B♭ in Dussek's Sonata in E♭, Op. 75. In Dussek's Sonatas and Concertos, which are of very unequal merit, you will find many beauties, real emanations of genius, inspirations; but with, however, not only some grammatical faults,

258   LECTURES ON MUSICAL ANALYSIS.   [LECT.

but also faults of structure, such as modulating into the original key in the course of the development, &c., and not unfrequent monotony. This is what I meant by speaking of him in the first Lecture as a *genius* but not a *master*. But by all means enjoy the exuberance of his sentiment, the richness of beautiful melody: " a prodigal," I think Mendelssohn called him.

Beethoven, in some of his *Rondos*, has furnished specially beautiful examples of this *rounded* structure, resulting so much from the nature of the *Subject*, the manner of its commencement: most of all, perhaps, in that of his Sonata Op. 7, the first Movement of which is quoted, Ex. 149. This *Rondo*, commencing so insinuatingly, with Dominant 7th harmony (Ex. 335), is singularly felicitous, even for

(335) *Poco Allegretto e grazioso.*

Beethoven, in the resumption of the *Subject;* but this felicity is only to be observed in listening to the whole Movement: no mere quotation of the returning point, the meeting-place of *Episode* and *Subject*, can impress you adequately. There is a *second Subject*, after the manner of a first Movement (Ex. 336), in the key of the Dominant; and when this closes, a " poising " passage on that Dominant harmony (Ex. 337) leads to the F as a little climax, and so the *Subject* is resumed. Instead of the whole of it being

repeated, however, it is interrupted on the Dominant (Ex. 338), and, by a simple change to B♮, C minor is reached,

for a stormy *Episode*, in marked contrast to the tenderness of the *first Subject*. This *Episode* closes in its own key, and then is projected or prolonged into another "poising" passage, the B♮ of C minor being, by *implied enharmonic*, treated as C♭, Minor 9th, to the Dominant of E♭; and so the return is again made to the original *Subject*. The *second Subject* (see Ex. 336) is then taken in this same key, as in a first Movement. The *first Subject* is once more taken; and then an *arrest* made, after the manner of that by which C minor was reached in Ex. 338; but this time, by another *implied* enharmonic, the B♭ being treated as A♯, leading to B♮, the very remarkable brief transition is made to the key of E♮, in which the first phrase of the *Subject* is taken. (Ex. 339.) By yet another implied enharmonic, B♮

being treated as C♭ (Ex. 340), the return is made, and an exquisite *Coda*, with *demi-semiquaver* movement, like the

(340)

C minor *Episode*, most joyously placid, however, not stormy, brings the Movement to a conclusion.

The 7th bar of the second part of the C minor *Episode* appears thus in most copies (Ex. 341), the last group being

(341)

unlike the corresponding bars in its figure; for Beethoven's then available compass was only up to F. It is no *liberty* to take with the composer's work, but the carrying out of his manifest intention, to begin that last group with G; and the most reverent editor might direct it to be so engraved.

The returns to the *Subject* are also particularly happy in the *Rondos* of his Sonatas Op. 22, Op. 26, and others which you can discover for your own enjoyment. That of Op. 22 is also noticeable for the embellishments and varied aspects of the *Subject*, on its different appearances. (See my *Text-book*, page 214.)

In the *Rondo* of his Op. 2, No. 2, another instance of implied enharmonic modulation occurs. (The first Movement is referred to in Lecture III.) In bar 2, the first C♯ is treated as D♭, Minor 9th to the Dominant of F♮. (Ex.

342.) In the return to A major, through B minor, the enharmonic B♭, A♯ is expressed. (Ex. 343.)

(342) *Grazioso.*

&c.

(343)

sf &c.

In the *Rondo* of Op. 28 (for other Movements see Lectures VIII. and IX.) a very interesting *Contrapuntal Episode* claims your attention. The *Theme* is *Imitational* in three parts (Ex. 344.) The *highest* part is then taken,

(344) *Allegro ma non troppo.*

pp &c.

with changed pitch, as the *middle* part (Ex. 345); then as

(345)

the *lowest* part, with changed, but still mutually imitational upper parts (Ex. 346); then in the *Minor mode*, as the highest part, with added 3rds, &c. (Ex. 347.)

(346)

(347)

This closely knit, but not at all pedantic *Episode*, with the rhythmical impulse kept up, is in capital contrast with the gaiety of the rest of the Movement. The *motivo*, moreover, may be considered as drawn from the *Subject* inversely:

the bracketed notes of Ex. 348, which, again, are presented

in, as it seems, *carillon* character, *i. e.* like a set of bells. (Ex. 349.)

His Op. 31, No. 1, has *two Rondos*, the *Adagio grazioso* and the *Finale*, which latter is expressly termed *Rondo*, and is worthy of much attention, both for the beauty of its ideas and for its *roundness* of *structure*. (The first Movement has been commented on in Lecture III.) The *Subject* (Ex. 350), specially adapted for the *return*, is taken in the left-

hand, with triplets superposed. (Ex. 351.) The second division of the *Subject* has a beautiful *counter-theme* in (as we may term it) the *Tenor* (Ex. 352); afterwards, with modification, the two themes are inverted. (Ex. 353.) In the second part of the Movement, after the first return to the

Subject, the *Episode* is of the nature of *development*. The Subject is answered *canonically*, though the *Canon* is not continued strictly. (Ex. 354.) The theme quoted in Ex. 352 is taken, on a Dominant pedal, as the commencement of

a lengthened *Coda*, and a contrapuntal part added. (Ex. 355.)

These are a few of the interesting points in this joyous *Rondo*. My object in all these talks is to lead you to observe, think, and analyse for yourselves: not to draw up a series of analytical programmes, or a set of complete analyses. You will find abundant material in the *Rondos* by Beethoven that I have not referred to, as well as in those that I have only partly analysed. I may just refer to one of the two *Rondos*, Op. 51 (not in the Sonatas). No. 2, in G (Ex. 356), has an *Episode* in a *different time* from the

rest of the *Rondo*, as well as in the key of E major, an unusual key, with regard to its relationship with the original key. (Ex. 357.) The other portion of the *Rondo* is very

much like a first Movement in its general structure: there being a *second Subject* in the *Dominant*, afterwards appearing in the original Tonic.

The *Finale* of Beethoven's String Trio, Op. 9, No. 2, is a *Rondo*, the second *Episode* being of the nature of *development* of the previous material: there being, in the whole Movement, little departure from first Movement structure, but with the *first Subject* reappearing prior to that *second Episode*. The *Finales* of his Sestet for two horns and stringed instruments, Op. 81, his Quintet in E♭ for stringed instruments, Op. 4, and various other chamber works, are also of *Rondo* form.

You will readily understand how such "running passage" *Subjects* as that of the last Movement of Weber's Sonata Op. 24, known as "*Il Moto continuo*," and the "*Perpetuum Mobile*" of Herz, and the similarly named (posthumous) piece by Mendelssohn, lend themselves readily to the structure that we have been considering; the return being so easily effected. The charming little piece by Mendelssohn, Op. 16, known as the "*Rivulet*" or "*Streamlet*," is hardly a *Rondino*: there being only *one return* to the *Subject*, just as a first Movement has. This is also the case with Sterndale Bennett's *Rondo Piacevole*, Op. 25, and previously-mentioned *Rondeau à la Polonaise*, Op. 37. Their structure is that of a first Movement without a second part, or development. The *first Subject* reappears immediately (or nearly so) after the conclusion of the first part; the *second Subject* reappears, in the key of the *Tonic*, just as in a first Movement; and there is no further return (*Rondo*-wise) to the *first Subject*, to differentiate the pieces from first Movements. Of course this seeming misnaming of such pieces has nothing to do with their beauty. I would not so much as mention the matter if I thought it would lessen your interest in or enjoyment of them.

268   LECTURES ON MUSICAL ANALYSIS.   [LECT.

Moreover, an *episodical* Movement may be excellent music, as in the case of Dussek's "*La Consolation*," and other Movements to which I have referred, and yet not have the continuity, or *rounded* return, which seem to me to be suggested by the term *Rondo*. Were I to urge to the contrary, I should condemn myself: my own "*Allegretto alla Marcia*" consisting of a *Subject* in E (Ex. 358), an *Episode*

in A (Ex. 359), another *Episode* in C (Ex. 360), both

Episodes terminating in their respective keys, with short *Intermezzi* to lead back to the *Subject*, and then a *Coda*. Mendelssohn's *Wedding March* and *Athalie March* are of similar *episodical* structure.

Each of the recognized plans of Movement structure has its beauties and adaptabilities, and one may partly coalesce with the other. The one requirement in a work of Art, that

(360)

appertains to our present discussion, is that it shall have *design*: that it shall not be *random* work, nor *piece-work*, nor " patchy," but complete and coherent.

LECTURE XII.

THE CODA AND CODETTA. DEFINITION AND APPLICATION. SOMETIMES AN AFFIX, FOR CONFIRMATION OF THE KEY. EXTENSION OF PLAGAL CADENCE. SOMETIMES A REMINISCENCE. SOMETIMES OCCURRING AT THE END OF THE FIRST PART. SOMETIMES FRESH WORKING SUGGESTED OR CONDENSED. CODA SOMETIMES AN EXTENSION OF PREVIOUS CODETTA. FINALE TO MOZART'S JUPITER SYMPHONY. SOMETIMES ENTIRELY FRESH MATERIAL.

XII.

I HAVE several times alluded to the *Coda* of a Movement. What is a *Coda?* The word means a *tail*, or tail-piece: from the Latin. It has, therefore, been applied as a musical term to a portion of a Movement added after that which seems to be the termination.

But it is not always merely an extension, an addition, an appendix: not merely *ornamental*, but often *rhetorical*, *structural*, or *logical*. It may, indeed, simply give finish more complete and decisive than the cadence or close by itself would do. But it is not a superfluity, or excrescence.

Sometimes, indeed, it is so short as to be termed only a *Codetta*, i. e. a *little* tail-piece. It serves, then, to avert abruptness, or indecision, by lingering on the *Tonic*, or other key-indicating harmonies. Even the *Plagal Cadence*, after the *Perfect*, or *full-close*, may be regarded as a *Codetta* for confirmation. Still more, such a little passage as occurs on a *Tonic-Pedal Bass*, after the cadence of the slow Movement of Haydn's Sonata No. 34 (see Examples 249, 250). In this there is a momentary modulation suggested to the *key* of the *Sub-dominant*, which is, as it were, an extension of the idea of the *Plagal Cadence;* but it is here *followed* by the *Dominant* harmony, as though for yet further confirmation of the original key, in contradiction to the suggested modulation. (Ex. 361.)

This suggestion of the Sub-dominant key, especially, as in this instance, upon a *Tonic-Pedal*, is a frequent incident in a *Coda;* the *Pedal-point* itself being confirmatory. (See

T

my *Text-book*, § 396.) Of this kind of *Coda*, instances abound in Bach's Preludes and Fugues, &c. The last six bars of the slow Movement of Beethoven's Sonata Op. 31, No. 2 (Ex. 362), constitute a *Coda* in which the *Plagal Cadence* is extended, and then followed by *Dominant* and *Tonic* harmonies, all on a *Tonic-Pedal*. The *Coda* (expressly so termed) to the *Minuet* of his Sonata No. 3, of the same

opus (Ex. 363), is also an *extended Plagal Cadence*, founded

on the opening of the second part of the *Minuet*. (Ex. 364.)

276   LECTURES ON MUSICAL ANALYSIS.   [LECT.

Sometimes the *Codetta* is less of the nature of a *confirmation*—more of that of a *reminiscence*, or "last fond look" at the *Subject*, or some phrase in the Movement. Thus, the slow Movement of Mozart's Sonata No. 5 commences (Ex. 365). The *Codetta* consists of a presentation

of this theme with different harmony. (Ex. 366.) Again,

in the *Codetta* to the *Rondo* of his Sonata No. 7 (see Example 298, &c.), the reminiscence is combined with the *Plagal Cadence*, and slight prolongation on a *Tonic-Pedal*. (Ex. 367.)

The *Coda* to the *Rondo* of Beethoven's Sonata Op. 7, referred to in the last lecture, takes the figure of the principal *Episode*, and invests it with new charm in the Major Mode, though without special working. Just such a lingering, drawing out of a previous figure, is to be observed in the

CODA LIKE A FAREWELL.

(367) *Allegretto grazioso.*

Coda to the first Movement of his Sonata Op. 14, No. 2. Such *Codas* are not mere *tags*, they are rather like "more last words," a lingering farewell: as Byron says—

"Farewell! a word that must be, and hath been :
A sound which makes us linger ;—yet—farewell."

Another such instance is at the end of the slow Movement in F of Mozart's Sonata No. 10 in C, which is of the nature of a reminiscence in the *Major Mode*, of the theme of the *Episode*, which was in the *Minor Mode;* a readjustment, moreover, of the *Codetta*, which was at the end of that *Episode*. (See page 212.)

See also the *Coda*, expressly so termed, to the *Rondo alla Turca* of Mozart's Sonata No. 11; the last eight bars of *both* parts of the first Movement of his Sonata No. 12 in F; also the slow Movement in B♭ of the same.

In fact, many *first parts*, and many Movements, after the cadence which would terminate the portion or the Movement, have a *Codetta*, just for greater satisfaction in impressing the key on the mind; such *Codetta* being derived either from some material in the Movement, which is, perhaps, most usual, or quite new.

Codettas of this kind, drawn from the previous material, occur at the end of both parts of the last Movement of Beethoven's Sonata Op. 2, No. 1 (commencing eight bars before the double-bar); first Movement of Op. 2, No. 2, both parts; Op. 10, No. 1, both parts; Op. 22, first Movement, both parts; slow Movement, both parts, &c.

Sometimes, however, there is a *Coda* at the *end of a Movement*, either quite new, or an extension of that which has appeared at the end of the first part. There is a beautiful instance at the end of the first Movement of Beethoven's small Sonata Op. 49, No. 1. The *Codetta* of four bars at the end of the first part is founded on the *second Subject*. (See page 64.) This, at the end of the Movement, is expanded into an *imitational* passage on the same theme. (Ex. 368.) These instances present the

Codetta as an *affix* to the conclusion of a Movement, or of a complete part of a Movement.

But then the very word *conclusion* may imply much more than the *cessation* or *termination* in point of time or continuity—more than the close or end. When the writer of the book of Ecclesiastes said, " Let us hear the conclusion of the whole matter," he meant that which was the outcome of his related experience. The *Coda* of his book was, " Fear God, and keep His commandments." As the revised version has it : " This is the end of the matter : all hath been heard." This is just what the beginning of the *Coda* in a musical Movement seems to say : " All hath been heard : this is the end of the matter." A *conclusion* is not merely an end by lapse of time, but a result arrived at by reasoning. So that, you see, this elevates a *Coda* into an important position above that of a mere affix : it may be a concentration or condensation of that which has been in the Movement, with perhaps, additional considerations, a *review*. When it comes at the end of a Fable, we call it the *Moral*. When it is the conclusion of a speech or oration, it is called the *Peroration*. And a *Coda*, in this sense, is a bringing together, as to a focus, the rays from the Movement. It takes, in a *Fugue*, the form of a *Stretto*, often on a *Tonic-Pedal:* a *Stretto* being the bringing into narrower compass, closer contact, or *straits*, the Subject and Answer, or portions of them. In a *Novel* or *Drama*, the same sort of process takes place when, as we say, towards the end, *the plot thickens*. Sometimes, indeed, the *Coda* is a very condensed, almost hasty, or at least impetuous, summing up. As in the case of that to Mozart's Sonata No. 14, first Movement. (See Lectures IV. and VI.) The working in the *second part* may have been, supposably, of the nature of *dilation:* that of the *Coda* will be, probably, pithy, or at least concise, compendious ; and, perhaps, with some brief hints of possible workings, which have not been carried out in the Movement.

Take, for an example, the first Movement of Beethoven's

Sonata Op. 2, No. 3. The *Coda* is inaugurated by an *interrupted cadence* (Ex. 369); the chord of A♭ instead of

(369) *Allegro con brio.*

the *Tonic* chord. This is followed by Arpeggios on the harmonies thus represented (Ex. 370): a relief from the

(370)

working, leading to a *Cadenza* (ornamental passage), drawn from the *Subject*, which is then returned to. Then, instead of this passage, which appeared at the opening of the Movement (Ex. 371), the figure marked * is worked imitationally,

(371)

thus (Ex. 372); and then the Movement is terminated in the same manner as the first part.

(372)

Another example is furnished by the first Movement of Beethoven's Sonata Op. 7. This *Coda*, also, is introduced by an *interrupted cadence*, just at the point where, in the first part, the close was made. (Ex. 373.) Then, among

(373) *Allegro molto con brio.*

other fresh presentations, this (Ex. 374) is thus changed

(374)

(Ex. 375). Afterwards occur some prolongations; and this

passage (Ex. 376), which would be perplexing to analyze

XII.] CODAS BY MOZART, BEETHOVEN, ETC. 283

except with this changed notation, and the harmonies indicated by the figuring. (Ex. 377.) The very vagueness

of the incomplete harmony, however, constitutes one of its charms.

I called your attention, in the last lecture, to the fine *Coda* of this kind, *i.e.* with suggestions of new working, &c., in the *Rondo* of Mozart's Sonata No. 15. Also, in Lecture VIII., to that of Mozart's Quintet in G minor. (Ex. 242.) Mozart's Quartets, &c. have various interesting examples of *Codas* in which some new bringing together of Subjects, or other workings, occur.

One of the most notable of *Codas*, for bringing together, in *Stretto* fashion, of Subjects previously presented in their simplicity, is that to the last Movement of Mozart's Symphony No. 41, the *Jupiter* (Ex. 378); and these Subjects, moreover, are in invertible Counterpoint with one another. This has often been adduced as a famous specimen of *Quintuple Counterpoint*. One inversion is (Ex. 379).

The *Coda* to the *Finale* of Beethoven's Sonata Op. 57 consists of an Episode of eighteen bars, commencing (Ex. 380), followed by a reiteration of some of the material of the Movement.

The *Coda* to the *Finale* of Mendelssohn's Scotch Symphony

is an appendix—a new theme, in fact, in different time ($\frac{3}{4}$) to that ($\frac{2}{4}$) of the Movement which it terminates.

Thus we have seen that a *Codetta* may be merely a short passage to give completeness to the termination of a Movement—an affix. Or it may be a *reminiscence* ere closing. Or, assuming the proportions of a *Coda*, it may, at the climax or peroration of the Movement, be a condensation or summing up, or concise bringing together, in some new way,

(379)

(380) *Presto.*

of the material, or some of it, which has appeared in the Movement. By no means is it, as a non-musical dictionary says, a passage *which may usually be omitted at pleasure!*

LECTURE XIII.

THE SONATA A DEVELOPMENT OF THE SUITE, PARTITA, OR LESSON. ORIGINALLY A SERIES OF DANCE-MOVEMENTS, WITH SOME OTHER FORMS. SURVIVAL OF THE MINUET. TRIO EXPLAINED. THE SCHERZO. UNION OF THE TWO STRUCTURES, CONTINUITY AND EPISODE, IN THE MINUET AND TRIO. CONCISE EXAMPLES, FROM HAYDN AND BEETHOVEN. MORE EXTENDED AND DEVELOPED EXAMPLES, BUT WITH COMPRESSED WORKING, FROM BEETHOVEN AND MOZART. RHYTHMICAL DEVICES. EXAMPLES FROM QUARTETS BY HAYDN, MOZART, AND BEETHOVEN. CONTRAPUNTAL, FUGAL, AND CANONIC DEVICES. EXAMPLES FROM DUSSEK, CLEMENTI, ETC.

XIII.

THE series of Movements constituting one complete work which we term a *Sonata* (from *Suonare* to sound), or *Symphony* (sounded together), or *Concerto* (consort of sounds),—these two latter terms being applied to music for several instruments,—originated in the *Suite de Pieces*, set of pieces, or Movements; or *Partita*, a composition divided into *parts*, or movements. The distinction between the *Suite* and the *Partita* seems not very clearly defined. According to some, *Partita* was the original German name, *Suite* the French term, and *Lesson* the English. Handel's *Suites* were originally called "*Lessons* for the Harpsichord." One great distinction between those forms of composition and our modern *Sonata* is that, in those, all the Movements had the same *Tonic* and *mode;* whereas in our *Sonatas,* &c., nearly always one, at least, of the Movements, is in a different key, or Mode, or both; which is a great advantage and relief. The old *Suites*, moreover, were made up, principally, of the *Dance-measures* of the period; though there were also Movements of another kind, as *Preludes*, *Airs*, with or without *Variations*, *Fugues*, &c. These dances having, for the most part, become obsolete, so have the musical Movements to which they were danced; though many writers of the present day produce compositions, ostensibly in the old idiom: rarely, however, including them in *Sonatas* or *Symphonies*. The *Minuet* is the only one of the old dance-measures which has been perpetuated as a Movement in a large work. The word is from *Menu* (Fr.), small, pretty, dainty, having reference to

U

the little steps taken in the dance, which was of French origin. Originally a sedate, dignified dance, the musical Movement had that character, as in the *Minuet* in Handel's *Overture* to *Samson*, and that in Mozart's *Don Giovanni*. There are several examples, moreover, in the *Suites* and *Partitas* by Bach. A *second Minuet* was also alternated, sometimes, with the first. This second Minuet was played by three instruments, the first, originally, for two: and thus the *second Minuet* was also sometimes termed the *Trio*. And this came to be the term applied to the *Episode*, or *Alternativo*, of other dance-measures. Haydn, in his *Symphonies* and *Quartets*, extended the *Minuet* from its original limited dimensions; and imparted to it a more jovial character, thereby abandoning all idea of adaption to dancing purposes. Some of his *Minuets*, indeed, are what were afterwards termed *Scherzos*. The term *Scherzo*, meaning joke, or play, was used, indeed, by Bach, for a Movement in $\frac{2}{4}$ time in his *third Partita*, in A minor. But Beethoven seems to have been the first to apply the term to an extended and quick Movement in triple time, taking the place, in a *Sonata*, or similar work, of the old *Minuet*. He, indeed, also applied the term to a Movement in $\frac{2}{4}$ time, of regular " continuity " plan, that in A♭, in his *Sonata* Op. 31, No. 3; which, however, is *followed* by a *Minuet* (see Examples 363, 364), and, therefore, does not take the place of one. Mendelssohn, again, used the term *Scherzo* for the lighter Movements taking the place of the *Minuet*, in various works; and you will remember his *Scherzo*, in $\frac{3}{8}$ time, in the *Midsummer Night's Dream* music. Indeed, he seems to have associated the term very much with fairy revels. There is nothing in the term itself which indicates the rhythm in which it is written: it is quite indefinite. Whereas a *Minuet* must be in triple time.

A *Minuet* and *Trio*, with *Da Capo*, and with or without *Codetta*, constitute one Movement, uniting the two structures of *Continuity* and *Episode:* the *Minuet* and the *Trio* each, in miniature, forming, in many cases, a complete little Movement on the plan of a first Movement. Some *Trios*, however, are not quite complete; having no full-close, but having a conducting passage to effect the return to the *Minuet*. These remarks apply equally to the quick Minuet termed a *Scherzo*, with *Trio*.

Some *Minuets*, indeed, are of such concise form, and so brief, as not even to modulate in the *first part*, but to make a *half-close* only; as that of Haydn's Sonata No. 7, in E (Ex. 381); or a *full-close* in the key, as that of his Sonata No. 31 (Ex. 382), in C♯ minor.

The *Minuet* of Beethoven's Sonata Op. 31, No. 3, already referred to (see Ex. 363, 364), has no modulation, the *first part* having only a *half-close, on* the *Dominant harmony*, not *in* the *key* of the Dominant.

The *Minuets* of his Sonatas Op. 10, No. 3, and Op. 22, and the *Scherzo* of Op. 26, terminate the *first part* with a *Perfect Cadence* in the key of the Movement.

The middle Movement, *Allegretto*, of his so-called "*Moonlight*" Sonata, Op. 27, No. 2, which is not termed either *Minuet* or *Scherzo*, but has a *Trio*, with *Da Capo*, is exceptional in its commencement. The first phrase is in A♭, the dominant to the key of the Movement, D♭; but the *first part* finishes in D♭, as does that of the *Trio*.

The *Allegretto* of his Sonata Op. 14, No. 1, likewise terminates the *first part* in the *Tonic*.

But, in other cases, and more frequently, the *Minuet* or *Scherzo* is of the structure of a very short first Movement, with, if not a *second Subject* in, at least a *modulation* to the *Dominant* or other related key; and with a *second part* in which more or less working is presented. From the limited dimensions of the Movement, however, it is obvious that not only must the *Subjects* themselves be brief and concise, but, also, the working, very terse, almost epigrammatic. If *Scherzo* means *pleasantry, fun*, a Movement of the kind that we are considering must, almost of necessity, illustrate the adage that "brevity is the soul of wit." All must be crisp and neat.

XIII.] FRAGMENTARY WORKING : BEETHOVEN'S OP. 2, NO. 1. 293

There is special opportunity and fitness in these little Movements, with short phrases, for fragmentary, I might say fractional, working; and for quaint and broken rhythmical effects.

Thus, the first phrase of Beethoven's Sonata Op. 2, No. 1, besides the incident of the bass of the second and third bars being the inverse of the highest part (Ex. 383), and appearing

afterwards with that highest part as an inner part,—very slight matters, doubtless (Ex. 384),—gives rise to the responses

by contrary motion, in these ways. (Ex. 385.) And the slight

294   LECTURES ON MUSICAL ANALYSIS.   [LECT.

form of the close (Ex. 384) suggests this bold passage to return to the *Subject*. (Ex. 386.) These are just the elements

of the homogeneity in the Movement, in which there is not an irrelevant bar: no "padding." In the *Trio* to this *Minuet*, the inversion of the parts can hardly escape your notice.

The imitational working in the *Scherzo* of No. 3 of the same *Opus* is very obvious and interesting. (Ex. 387.) And observe, also, how the original figure of the *Subject* is thus varied in presentation (Ex. 388); and afterwards used for the *Codetta* to the *Scherzo;* and finally in altered guise for

the *Coda* to the entire Movement. (Ex. 389.) Take, as an

example of compact structure and neat working, the single *Minuet*, without *Trio*, of Mozart, commencing (Ex. 390). The last two bars of this extract are reiterated so as to effect a modulation; and the passage commencing (Ex. 391) occupies the position of *Codetta*. In the second part (Ex. 392), that which may be called the Tenor of bars 5 and 6 (Ex. 390), and which is an extension of the bass of the opening bars, is, with modification, taken by inverse Movement, in

296   LECTURES ON MUSICAL ANALYSIS.   [LECT.

(390)

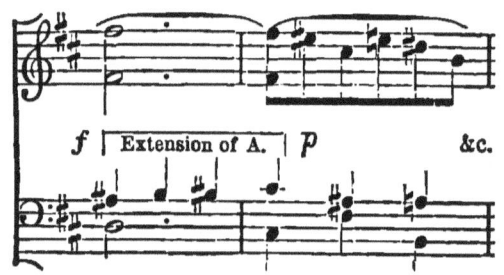

(391)

(392)

MOZART'S MINUETS.

Prolongation. &c.

thirds, initiated with a forcible discord; and the bass has a contrapuntal passage, partly suggested, it would seem, by the last group of bar 2 (Ex. 391). This semiquaver figure is prolonged as indicated, and leads to the return of the *Subject*. This is accompanied by the figure of the inner parts of bar 2, Example 392, by *retrograde* and *inverse* movement, answered in the bass. (Ex. 393.) The Movement then proceeds as in

(393)

&c.

the first part, terminating in the original Tonic. This Minuet is singularly bright and interesting, needing and repaying study as a whole.

One of the most notable of *Minuets* is that, with *Trio*, in Mozart's Symphony in G minor, No. 40. This is remarkable, not only for the stately dignity of the *Minuet*, and the simple sweetness of the *Trio*, but also for its *rhythm*, for its *working*, and for the *Codetta* of the *Minuet*. The rhythm of the opening is of three bars, there being three phrases of that length, followed by two phrases of a bar each, and one more three-bar phrase. Slight deviations from the exactitude of these proportions will be observed; the third phrase lacking one beat, and the last phrase having an extra beat. (Ex. 394.) The second part

(394) *Allegro.*

continues the three-bar rhythm; the *Subject* being taken as the bass, with a new figure superposed. (Ex. 395.) This

(395)

&c.

being reiterated twice, and followed by one-bar phrases, leads to the return of the *Subject;* but with quite new presentation, the imitational working involving, or overlapping the rhythm, and intertwining the parts. (Ex. 396.) Then follows the

(396)

Codetta: two three-bar phrases, with reharmonizing of the *Subject.* (Ex. 397.)

(397)

The *Trio* contrasts with the *Minuet*, firstly, in being in the Major Mode; secondly, in its rhythm of three phrases of two bars, followed by four phrases of two bars, &c.; and, thirdly, in the quiet, and fascinating instrumentation. (Ex. 398.)

(398)

Much of the charm felt in listening to such a work is often due to exquisite contrivances like these rhythmical changes, which avert squareness, while preserving balance and proportion. The effect is recognized, but the causes are not apprehended.

The brevity of *Minuets* and *Scherzi* affords opportunity for quaint fancies, almost to be termed *Jeux d'Esprit*, which would hardly warrant pursuing to greater length than the limits of a short movement. Thus, in Haydn's Quartet in D, for stringed instruments, the *Minuet* is "*alla Zingarese:*" that is, in the style (and rhythm) of a gipsy song or dance. The *cross accents*, mixed among the parts, you will at once recognize; as well as the little close imitations. (Ex. 399.)

(399) *Allegretto.*

Again, in another Quartet, in G, the *Minuet* has a *first part* with two phrases of five bars each; the first being (Ex. 400).

(400) *Allegretto.*

&c.

The Minuet of Mozart's Quartet No. 10 has a *first part* with two phrases of seven bars each; the first being (Ex. 401).

(401) *Allegretto.*

&c.

Squareness is often averted by the two phrases of the first part being of different lengths: one of four bars, the other of six; as in another Quartet (Ex. 402) of Haydn's.

On the other hand, when the rhythm is exactly equal in the first part, it is varied, or broken, in the second part. By *broken rhythm* is meant the breaking off before a phrase is

(402) *Presto.*

completed, or, in some way, abridging it: and, likewise, the not matching, by parallel phrases, but having phrases, or parts thereby, of different lengths, in succession. Also, there may be *overlapping* rhythm: one phrase beginning before another has terminated. All these contrivances and irregularities require nice adjustment, acute sense of proportion and balance, so that, amid all the irregularity, there shall be no *lopsidedness*.

The *Scherzo* of Beethoven's Quartet in F, Op. 18, No. 1 (Ex. 403), affords a beautiful example of varied rhythm.

&c.

The first part is in two-bar rhythm: the eight bars which would constitute the first section being prolonged to ten by a reiteration of the last two. Then the second part commences with two phrases of three bars each; followed by the resumption of the two-bar rhythm, and succeeded by various rhythmical and other devices.

The Quartets of Haydn contain many interesting examples of broken and varied rhythm, of which he was so great a master.

Sometimes *contrapuntal*, instead of *rhythmical*, devices are made the feature in Movements of this kind. Thus, Beethoven, in his Quartet in C minor, Op. 18, No. 4, commences the *Scherzo* after the manner of a *Fugue* opening; though not with a *Tonal*, but a *Real* answer: a distinction which some of you know about, but which I shall enter upon in another Lecture. (Ex. 404.) The Fugal working is

&c.

not kept up in any strict fashion; the *Scherzo* being in first Movement form. It takes the place of a slow Movement, being followed by a *Minuet* and *Trio*. Mendelssohn, and after him other composers, have written *Scherzi* with Fugal openings and free working. Beethoven himself, in his Symphony No. 1, in C, composed at about the same period as that at which he wrote the Quartets Op. 18, commences the slow Movement in the same fashion; but with a *Tonal* answer: *Tonic* for *Dominant*. (Ex. 405.) There is

(405) *Andante Cantabile con moto.*

a pleasant *naïveté* in introducing this semi-scholastic element into that which is intended as a comparatively light Movement: "playing at Fugue writing," it has been called by Professor Macfarren.

The *Minuet* of one of Haydn's Quartets in D minor is a strict two-part *Canon* between the violins in 8^{ves} and the viola and violoncello in 8^{ves}; commencing (Ex. 406).

(406) *Allegro, ma non troppo.*

The *Minuet* of Dussek's beautiful Sonata Op. 77, entitled "*L'Invocation,*" is a *Canon* in the 7th below, commencing (Ex. 407).

A *Canon* may seem to be, in the nature of the case, a most wilful bit of pedantry, and needless self-restriction, curbing all spontaneous working of the imagination. But, when associated, as in these Minuets, with definite, rhythmical Subjects, and orderly Movement structure, in brief development, so as not to become tedious, the ingenuity imparts a little life and interest to that which, after all, is intended as a relief from the more sustained attention which longer Movements require.

Similar examples are to be found in the Sonatas of Clementi. Thus, the *Minuet* of his Op. 40, No. 1, in G, is a *perpetual Canon* in the 8^{ve}, commencing (Ex. 408). And

(408) *Allegro.*

the *Trio*, or *Alternative Minuet*, is also a *Perpetual Canon* by *inverse movement*, commencing (Ex. 409).

(409)

The Minuet of Mozart's stringed instrument Quintet, No. 1 in C minor, is in Canon, during nearly all the *first part*, between the first violin and violoncello, with harmonies in the inner parts. (Ex. 410.) The Canon is resumed at the return of the *Subject*. The Trio, which is in Quartet only, the second Viola being *tacet*, has two Canons by *inverse movement;* one

(410)

XIII.]   MOZART'S QUINTET IN C MINOR.   309

&c.

between the two violins, and the other between the first viola and violoncello. (Ex. 411.)

(411)

The *Trio* to the *Scherzo* of Beethoven's Sonata in C minor, for pianoforte and violin, Op. 30, No. 2, has canonic device between the violin and the left-hand pianoforte part.

Thus, the kind of Movement which we have been considering may consist of the simplest dance-measure, unworked, or may be a concise Movement of development, or may be a presentation of compressed, terse, contrapuntal ingenuity.

Sometimes the Scherzando Movement is termed an *Intermezzo*: i. e. an intermediate Movement. In Beethoven's Sonata Op. 101, a Movement "*alla Marcia*" takes the place of the *Scherzo*. Similar exceptions will be met with.

LECTURE XIV.

FUGUE. GENERAL REMARKS ABOUT THE STYLE. DEFINITION. THE SUBJECT: WHEREIN DIFFERENT FROM SONATA SUBJECT. SIMPLE, OR TWOFOLD. THE ANSWER : REAL OR TONAL. PLAGAL ANSWER TO AUTHENTIC SUBJECT, AND VICE VERSÂ. COUNTERPOINT, OR COUNTER-SUBJECT. EXPOSITION. EPISODES. WORKING OF THE MATERIAL ANNOUNCED IN THE EXPOSITION. THE STRETTO. IRRELEVANCY DEPRECATED. VARIOUS FUGAL DEVICES. TWO-PART FUGUE IN C MINOR: THREE-PART FUGUE IN D MINOR: FOUR-PART FUGUE IN G MINOR, ALL BY BACH, ANALYSED. UNEXPECTED ENTRIES. ILLUSTRATIONS FROM MOZART'S PIANOFORTE DUET FUGUE IN F MINOR. EXTRANEOUS MODULATION. HANDEL'S FUGUE IN B MINOR.

XIV.

WE now come to the consideration of one of the noblest forms of composition, structurally viewed: that of FUGUE. It is a style which has suffered much, and been disesteemed by shallow musicians, because of the dry pedantry with which it has been encrusted and encumbered. And it has been more or less discarded by some, because of the lack of that peculiar power or faculty of close thinking which is requisite for its pursuit and study. Moreover, the extreme rarity of that union of faculties which can combine exact thinking with vivid imagination, and animate structural strictness with life, has occasioned the undeniable result that a large number of Fugues are exceedingly dry, square, stiff, and pedantic. Just as the Budget speeches of one eminent Chancellor of the Exchequer have been informed by such intellectual grace as to invest figures and calculations with charm, so some great musicians have, as it were, almost revelled in their bonds when writing under the restrictions, voluntarily submitted to, of the Fugue style and structure; and have presented Fugues, not as displays of scholastic attainment, but as manifestations of intellectual power, mental force. In a Fugue, a composer appears as a man of one idea: not because he is narrow, contracted, but because that one idea possesses, inspires, animates him. In a Fugue, a composer does not relate a history, or present various incidents in dramatic form; but expounds a text, lays down a thesis, and elaborates and illustrates it: conducts an argument.

A *Fugue* is a composition in which a *Subject* or *Theme* is announced in one part, reiterated or answered in the other parts, successively, and imitationally worked in whole or sectionally, with little or no intermission throughout the Movement. Some Fugues have two Subjects announced simultaneously, or nearly so, and worked together; constituting a *Double Fugue*. Sometimes, after a Fugue has proceeded for some time with one Subject, a new Subject is introduced, and worked, either at first independently, or at once in conjunction with the *first Subject*. Such a Fugue is, by some musicians, termed a *Fugue with two Subjects;* though, ultimately, it becomes a *Double Fugue*. There may be more than two Subjects thus introduced, as in No. 4 of Bach's *Das Wohltemperirte Clavier*. (See my *Text-book*, § 395.)

But a *Fugue Subject* differs from a *Sonata Subject*, such as we considered in the earlier Lectures, in being, in the first instance, *unharmonized:* a Subject of single notes, the harmony being *implied* instead of *expressed*, as in all proper melodies. Also, in being short, terse, self-contained; and yet suggestive of elaboration. A *Sonata Subject* may, as we have seen, be of considerable extent, from eight bars to much greater length; whereas a *Fugue Subject* rarely exceeds eight bars: in fact, rarely extends to that number, sometimes consisting of four or five notes, as we shall see. While a *Sonata Subject* is more frequently rhythmically divisible, like the lines of a stanza in verse; a *Fugue Subject* is like an *apophthegm*, concise and sententious. It may be one simple idea, like the assertion, "All the world's a stage," or it may be twofold, as when to that assertion is added, "and all the men and women merely players." In any case it needs to be crisp and epigrammatic, like a definite proposition, that is to be proved: easily recognizable at every recurrence throughout the Fugue. Of the Simple Subject, that of the *Finale* of Mozart's 1st Quartet furnishes an example. (Ex. 412.) Also, the chorus, "And with His

(412) *Molto Allegro.*

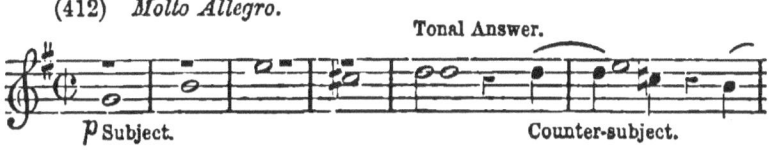

stripes," in ·Handel's "*Messiah.*" Or that in Mozart's "*Jupiter*" Symphony, quoted in Examples 378, 379. Of twofold Subjects, take, for example, No. 16 of Bach's *Das Wohltemperirte Clavier* (Ex. 413), and No. 2 of Mendels-

(413)

sohn's Op. 35, though so short (Ex. 414), and No. 6 of the same set (Ex. 415).

When a *Fugue Subject* has been announced by one voice,

(414)

(415) *Allegro con brio.*

or in one part, it is immediately *answered* in another part: the *Answer* being, generally speaking, the *transposition* of the *Subject* into the *key of the Dominant*: either a 5th higher or a 4th lower. This is the general definition of the *Answer*, which is then termed a *real* Answer, and the *Fugue* with such an Answer, a REAL FUGUE. This is exemplified in the *Answer* to the *Subject* in Example 414. The Answer to Example 415 is also real. When, however, the *Subject* has the *Dominant* of the key prominent, as a kind of boundary note, thus (Ex. 416, *a*, *b*), or as a

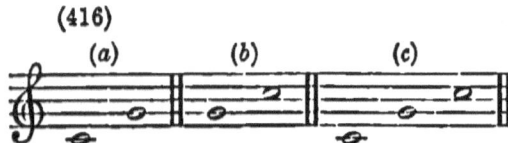

dividing note of the octave, thus (*c*), the *Answer* will be somewhat modified, and will be termed *Tonal*, and the *Fugue* with such an Answer, a TONAL FUGUE. The old rule about such Answers was that a *Subject* in the *Authentic Mode*—i. e. lying principally between the *Tonic* and its 8^{ve}, or between the *Tonic* and the 5th above, must be answered in the *Plagal Mode*—i. e. between the *Dominant* and its 8^{ve}, or between the *Dominant* and the 4th above. And, in like manner, that a *Plagal* Subject must have an *Authentic*

Answer; the *Dominant*, moreover, answering the *Tonic*, and *vice versâ*, in all marked, prominent instances. This would obviously necessitate the alteration of some intervals of the *Subject* in the *Answer:* a 4th for a 5th, a 2nd for a 3rd, a repetition for a 2nd, and *vice versâ*.

In addition to this modification, derived from the old *Tonality*, similar alteration is necessary where a *Subject* modulates to the *Dominant:* the only completed (as distinct from transient) modulation, occurring in a *Fugue Subject*. The *Answer* must, in that case, to avoid wandering too far from the original key, modulate from the *Dominant* to the *Tonic*.

The laws that govern the tonal modification of a *Fugue Answer* are somewhat complex, and give trouble to learners. They are explained in considerable detail in my *Text-book;* and, since that was published, have been elucidated, still further, in the admirable *Primer* on *Fugue* by Mr. James Higgs. As I am now showing you, not how to write Fugues, but how to understand them, I do not reiterate those rules. Illustrations of their application will present themselves as we proceed.

The *Answer* commences either simultaneously with, or immediately after, the conclusion of the *Subject;* and, during that *Answer*, the part which announced the *Subject* proceeds with a *Counterpoint:* sometimes a *Double-Counterpoint*—i. e. *invertible*, so as to admit of its appearance either above or below the *Subject* or *Answer*, throughout the *Fugue;* in which case it is termed a *Counter-Subject:* a term loosely applied, however, to the Counterpoint, even when not appearing as the satellite of the Subject throughout the Fugue.

After the *Answer*, if the Fugue be in more than two parts, another part reiterates the *Subject*, sometimes after a brief parenthetical passage, or EPISODE; and the other parts continue in Counterpoint. If the Fugue be in four parts, the *Answer* again follows in that fourth part. When the parts have all made one announcement of the *Subject* or *Answer*, that which is termed the EXPOSITION is completed.

After the *Exposition*, the *Subject* and *Counterpoints* that have appeared therein are worked, with modulations, throughout the Movement. The working may be of the *Subject* in its entirety, or portions of it, in fragmentary workings, with *Episodes*, drawn from the *Subject*, or from one or more of the Contrapuntal figures that have appeared in the *Exposition;* which is, so to speak, the egg from which the Fugue is hatched. The power of the working consists in presenting the *Subject*, and other materials in the *Exposition*, in various phases, in different superpositions, and so on. Moreover, the *Subject* may be introduced by *inverse movement*, by *augmentation*, or by *diminution*.

One specialty of imitational working is of great importance in a Fugue: that of a STRETTO, which, as it is generally explained, is the bringing of the *Subject* and *Answer* closer together than in the first announcement; the imitation, or Answer, commencing before the termination of the Subject or antecedent. This general definition, however, is hardly adequate, if it is intended that the Subject and the *Answer a 5th above, or 4th below it*, are necessarily the two parts brought *close* (as the word *Stretto* means). The imitation in a *Stretto* may be at any interval, according to the susceptibilities of the Subject for such working. And, moreover, some Subjects admit of more *Stretti* than one: the imitating part commencing at different points in the Subject: and, sometimes, proceeding by inverse movement, by diminution, &c. It will be obvious that, for a Subject to be capable of this treatment by *Stretto*, it must include a *Canon*, more or less complete, within itself: the latter part of the Subject being in Counterpoint with the earlier part. Some Fugue

Subjects are rich in this respect: others admit of no *Stretto*.

There must be nothing *irrelevant* in a Fugue: no portion which is not in some way suggested by the *Exposition:* the Fugue being evolved from that as its germ. And, as there must be no digression, there must be no repetition: no restatement in the same way. Every time the *Subject* appears, it must be in some new aspect, with different contrapuntal accompaniment; or, if the same, it must be with different superposition of parts. And, in conjunction with, or including, the *Fugal* working, there will generally be an outline in the structure of the Movement, analogous to that of a Movement of continuity: a first part, with a more or less marked close in a relative key; then, closer, and fragmentary working, and a return to the key with the Subject by no means in the same mode of presentation as previously: and, finally, a working up, by intensified interest, perhaps by a *Dominant-Pedal-point*, followed by a *Tonic-Pedal-point* as a *Coda*. All this need not occur in every Fugue; but this summary will place before you *what to look for* in a Fugue: how to analyse it. First the *Subject* as a *Thesis*: whether the *Answer*, or *Antithesis*, should be *real* or *tonal*: whether, if tonal, it is *authentic* or *plagal*, and what the modifications are. Then the *Counterpoint:* whether *double* (invertible) or not: whether, therefore, it is a *Counter-Subject:* and whether, if *double-counterpoint*, it is in the 8ᵛᵉ only, or in the 10th or 12th likewise. Then all the various *superpositions* of the Subject and Counterpoints. And, further, what fugal devices are introduced, such as *Stretti*, augmentation, diminution, inverse movement, fragmentary working, episodes, and whence derived. And, over all, what is the general plan of the Movement, as regards modulations, &c. This, briefly, is how to analyse a Fugue. Now let us do it.

It may seem to you, as I have known it appear to some teachers, that a two-part Fugue offers so little scope for working, that not only must it be difficult to construct such a Fugue with any considerable development, but also that there can be little to learn from analysing such a Fugue. There is only one two-part Fugue in Bach's *Das Wohltemperirte Clavier*, No. 10, in E minor, which is analysed by Mr. Higgs in his *Primer*. We will take his single little Fugue in C minor, of only 27 bars length; the *Subject* being of three bars, announced in the Bass, and divisible into three figures. (Ex. 417.) The Dominant not being prominent, and no modulation occurring in the *Subject*, the *Answer*, in the Treble, is *real*. The *Subject* appears, entire, four times, including the *Answer*, which is its exact transposition: (1) alone, in Bass: (2) in Treble, with Counter-

(417)

XIV.] BACH'S TWO-PART FUGUE IN C MINOR. 321

point, in G minor: (3) similarly, with slight modification of Counterpoint, in F minor: (4) in Bass, with different Counterpoint, in C minor, commencing at the half-bar. Thus 12 bars of the 27 are occupied. The first *Episode* is entirely formed from the figures of the *Subject* and *Counterpoint*, as partly indicated in Example 417; and effects a modulation to E♭, in which key the first bar of the *Subject* enters, answered in the 8ᵛᵉ above: that figure being repeated, and a modulation effected to F minor, in which the above-mentioned appearance of the entire *Subject* occurs, soon followed by (Ex. 418); and then a brief prolongation leads

(418)

Y

, &c.

to the termination of the Fugue. There is neither double-Counterpart nor *Stretto*, though there is an *interruption* of the Subject by another entry; nor is there any inverse movement. But without any such devices, the continuity, relevancy, and interest are maintained without limp or halt throughout.

Take now a three-part Fugue (termed *Fughetta*, short Fugue), also by Bach, not from *Das Wohltemperirte Clavier*. The remarkably simple, and, as might be thought, unpromising *Subject* of even notes, announced in the middle part, has a *real Answer*, in the highest part, in A minor, in which key, also—contrary to usual custom—the next entry is made, in the Bass, thus completing the *Exposition*. (Ex. 419.)

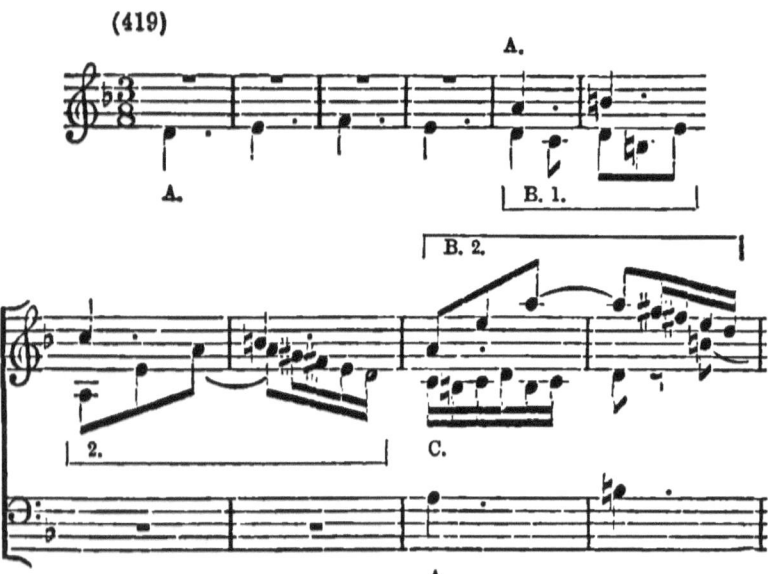

BACH'S THREE-PART FUGUE IN D MINOR.

The *Subject* and the two *Counterpoints* I have lettered respectively A, B, C, to assist in identification in their several superpositions. It will be seen in Examples 419, 420, 421, that the *Subject* A occurs 9 times in this Fugue of 57 bars length: once alone at the opening; twice as the upper of two parts—*i. e.* with B and D respectively: once as the lower of two parts—*i. e.* with D above it: three times as the lowest of three parts—different Contrapuntal

(421)

XIV.]   ESSENTIALS OF A FINE FUGUE.   325

superpositions, however : once as the highest of three parts ; and once as the middle part of three. There is neither inverse movement, nor *Stretto*, nor *Pedal-point;* and the only modulations are to A minor and G minor. That which I am directing your attention to, just now, is the application of Contrapuntal skill to the different superpositions of the *Subject* and *Counterpoints:* a most important and interesting matter for you to study in your analysis of Fugues. No Fugue can be worth much that does not furnish this material for your analysis ; while, if it does this, it may be a fine Fugue, without the devices of augmentation, diminutions, inverse movement, or even *Stretti*. Some Subjects are not susceptible of these ; but there *must* be the different presentations of the *Subject*, which I have thus far illustrated.

Take now a four-part Fugue, No. 16, of Bach's *Das Wohltemperirte Clavier* (Ex. 422), of which the *Subject* is given in Example 413. As this commences with the *Dominant*, the *Answer*, according to rule, commences with the *Tonic*, a 4th above the *Dominant*, and is *tonal;* and,

in compensation for that contracted distance, and in compliance with the requirement that the 6th to the Tonic shall be answered by the 6th to the Dominant, takes an ascent of a minor 3rd, instead of a minor 2nd, and then proceeds unaltered to the end. This *Subject*, formed, as I have said, of two figures, is well adapted, on that account, for *sectional* working; and it also affords opportunities for *Stretti*. The *Counter-Subject*, in double-counterpoint, which accompanies the *Answer*, commences with the second figure of the *Subject*, by inverse movement, which, occurring immediately afterwards in the *Answer*, keeps up the continuity; and, prolonged in the next bar, makes a good *Episode*, which is necessary before a satisfactory entry of the Subject in G minor can be made. This necessity is frequent, especially in Fugues in the minor mode, because the *minor* key of the

XIV.] BACH'S FUGUE NO. 16, IN G MINOR. 327

5th of the scale, in which the *Answer* appears, is not a true *Dominant* to the original key. (See Nos. 2, 6, 8, 14, &c: of *Das Wohltemperirte Clavier*.) At the fourth entry one of the parts ceases, so that the four parts do not appear simultaneously till bar 15. (Ex. 423.)

328　　LECTURES ON MUSICAL ANALYSIS.　　[LECT.

The *Episode* of four bars, commencing at the termination of the *Exposition*, bar 8, is formed from the second figure of the *Subject*, which, indeed, is almost unintermittently kept up throughout the Fugue. At bar 12 another series of entries commences in the key of B♭ major (Ex. 423), the intervals being changed from minor to major, &c. Notice that, the key of F being temporarily established, the third of these entries, at *, is in the *Subject* form, not that of the *Answer*. And that at †, which, moreover, is in Stretto with the bass, occurring when the key is changing to E♭, the fourth note is E♭, instead of being a leading-note, as in the original *Subject*. This kind of modification is frequent, for similar reasons, in the development of a Fugue. And then, two entries being made in C minor, bars 20, 21, the *Answer* in G minor, bar 23, makes the return, naturally, to that original key; the two forms of commencement being, so to speak, combined by the two semiquavers. Then follow the *Stretto* passages (Ex. 424), and two more entries (Ex. 425)

(424)

terminate the Fugue of 34 bars length, in which there are 13 entries of *Subject* or *Answer*, besides the *Stretto*. There is no *Pedal-point*. During a not inconsiderable portion only three parts are simultaneously at work: in the last two bars there

(425)

are five parts. The *Counter-Subject* is the invariable companion of the *Subject*, except in the last entry. To assist in study the *Subject* and *Answer* are marked ∧ and the *Counter-Subject* ⌒ in the Examples. All the entries should be compared, to enable you to appreciate the fertility of contrapuntal resource exhibited, in conjunction with entire naturalness. Besides the alternation of D minor with G minor in the *Exposition*, the modulations are to B♭, very transiently to E♭, and to C minor, followed by the return to the original key, which is not again quitted.

Unexpected entries, either before the termination of the *Subject*, that is, in *Stretto*, or at unlooked-for intervals, are among the interesting points, which give life to a Fugue; and this last-mentioned form of the unexpected may be most happily made the means of effecting modulation. A beautiful instance of this is furnished by Mozart's Fugue in F minor, from the Fantasia composed (1791) for a musical clock, known now as a pianoforte duet. The *Subject* and *tonal Answer* are (Ex. 426). After the *Exposition*, and a

(426) *Allegro.*

brief *Episode*, the *Subject* enters in B♭ *minor* (Ex. 427), and is answered in A♭ *major* (bar 4), answered in Stretto, bar 5,

XIV.] MOZART'S FUGUE IN F MINOR. 333

334 LECTURES ON MUSICAL ANALYSIS. [LECT.

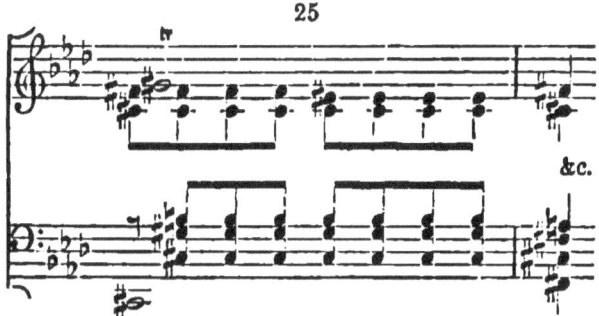

afterwards in D♭ *major* and E♭ successively, bars 8, 10. A fragmentary entry *by diminution* occurs, bar 9; and then the *Subject* by *inverse Movement*, in F minor, bar 13, &c. C minor being reached, by regular process, a most startling modulation is made, by an implied enharmonic, to the key of F♯ minor. The chord of the Augmented (German) 6th in C minor, bar 22, is changed, by the A♮, to the 1st inversion of the Diminished 7th, with D, the Supertonic, as its root (the G♭ in the highest part being used for convenience instead of F♯), and the E♭ and C♮ being really treated as D♯ and B♯, respectively, with G♯, Supertonic of F♯, as root, resolve on the harmony of that key, in its 2nd inversion. Although the immediate purpose for which I brought this Fugue to your notice was the modulation by unexpected answers, it is out of the question for me to pass by these other points that I have specified; especially this very remarkable modulation.

But, beyond all this, Mozart has displayed his marvellous fertility in that, after bringing the Fugue to this temporary termination, and returning to the *Subject* of the *Fantasia*, of which it forms a part, he proceeds to a lovely slow Movement in A♭; and then, returning again to the *Fantasia Subject* in F minor, re-introduces the Fugue in quite fresh guise, with new florid Counterpoint, thus (Ex. 428).

The general direction to students about Fugue writing is

to make only *natural*, as distinguished from *extraneous* modulation. But, as in other things, so here: genius has its prerogatives. Such instances as this just given, and of Handel's Fugue in E minor (*Suite* IV.), in the course of which the Subject is introduced in F♯ *minor*, are unprecedented, and not to be taken as precedents. They are inimitable, both because they *ought* not to be, and *cannot* be imitated with success.

Another instance of effecting a change of key by means

of an unexpected entry may be quoted from Handel's Fugue
in B minor, commencing (Ex. 429). In the course of the

Fugue this passage (Ex. 430) occurs, including a *Stretto*
between the extreme parts (for the time being), the Tenor
entering with the Subject two bars after its entry in the
Treble: the Subject being modified in this Treble entry, for
convenience, by the descent of a 3rd instead of the ascent

of a 6th. (See my *Text-book*, § 385.) Subsequently the Bass enters with the Subject in D major.

Another Stretto from the same Fugue is (Ex. 431), and illustrates the occasional alteration, in the course of a Fugue, of the length of the first note of the Subject. (See my *Text-book*, § 384.) The same kind of alteration may be found in Bach's Fugue in E♭, Vol. ii. of *Das Wohltemperirte Clavier*, No. 7.

(431)

LECTURE XV.

FUGUE, *continued*. UNEXPECTED ENTRIES OF SUBJECT OR ANSWER. COUNTER-EXPOSITION. VARIOUS ORDERS OF ENTRY. EXAMPLES FROM BACH AND MENDELSSOHN. BRIEF ANALYSIS OF BACH'S NO. 9 FROM 'DAS WOHLTEMPERIRTE CLAVIER.' EXCEPTIONAL ANSWERS: EXAMPLES FROM BACH AND DUSSEK. EPISODES IN FUGUES: WHEREIN DIFFERENT FROM THOSE IN RONDOS. INVERSE MOVEMENT. EXAMPLE, WITH STRETTI, FROM BACH, NO. 20. CANONIC STRETTO FROM HANDEL. EXAMPLE OF COUNTER-SUBJECT FROM HANDEL'S 'JUDAS MACCABÆUS.' BEAUTIFUL MANNER OF ENTRY THAT SHOULD CHARACTERIZE A FUGUE. INEXHAUSTIBLENESS OF THE TOPIC.

XV.

In the last Lecture I called your attention to the importance and power of unexpected entries, especially at unlooked-for intervals, so contrived as to effect modulation in conjunction therewith. This is specially to be noticed in connection with a section which, in some Fugues, follows the *Exposition*, and is termed the *Counter-Exposition*. This, as its name partly implies, is a reversal of the order of entry which has been adopted in the *Exposition*: the voices or parts which had the *Subject* now taking the *Answer*, and *vice versâ*, and the *Answer*, moreover, taking the lead, followed by the *Subject*, and so on. This latter order, however, is not always observed; nor, indeed, is the somewhat cumbersome process of a complete *Counter-Exposition* frequently to be found, especially in a *Fugue* of four or more parts. More usually, in a four-part *Fugue*, after the fourth entry, which has been of the *Answer*, in the *Dominant*, completing the *Exposition*, one more entry, in the *Tonic*, follows, and then divergence begins, by an entry in an unexpected interval and key, as in the *Fugue* by Mozart. (Ex. 426, 427, 428.) This is the order in Bach's *Das Wohltemperirte Clavier*, No. 5, in D major, the sixth, or *diverging* entry, as it may be designated, being in B minor: in No. 17, in A♭, the sixth entry being in F minor: in No. 41, &c. The fifth entry in the *Tonic* is especially desirable where the *Subject* has been entirely in that key; as, in such case, the fourth entry, being the *Answer* in the *Dominant*, needs the additional entry after the *Exposition*, in order to confirm the impression of the *Tonic*, before modulating.

In No. 1 of Bach's *Das Wohltemperirte Clavier*, however, the order of entry is *Subject, Answer, Answer, Subject;* the *Exposition* thus closing in the *Tonic:* followed instantly, not by any *Counter-Exposition*, but by close *Stretto* working. In No. 12, in F minor, the order of entry is *Subject, Answer, Subject, Subject.* In No. 4, in C♯ minor, a five-part *Fugue*, the fourth entry is, unusually, in the *Sub-dominant*, and then the final entry of the *Exposition* is in the *Tonic.*

In *Fugue* 10 of Bach's *Art of Fugue*, also, the first *Answer* commences in the key of the *Sub-dominant*. (Ex. 432.)

In Mendelssohn's organ *Fugue*, Op. 37, No. 3, the *Answer* commences *on* the *Sub-dominant*, not *in* the *key* of the *Sub-*

dominant,—although the *Subject* begins with the *Tonic:* this being inevitable if the form of the *Subject* is to be preserved. (Ex. 433.) Exceptional Subjects require excep-

(433)

tional treatment; but such instances are not to be taken as precedents, to warrant looseness in treatment on the part of young writers. I do not justify these instances as right because Bach and Mendelssohn wrote them. They wrote them because they were right.

In Bach's three-part *Fugue* in E, No. 9 of *Das Wohltemperirte Clavier*, the *Subject* is announced in the Alto, the real *Answer* made in the Treble, and the *Subject* again enters in the Bass. (Ex. 434.) That which serves as *Counter-*

(434)

344　LECTURES ON MUSICAL ANALYSIS.　[LECT.

XV.] BACH NO. 9. EXCEPTIONAL ANSWERS. 345

Exposition follows, one bar after the close of the *Exposition*; and consists of *Subject* in the Treble, *Answer* in the Alto, and then *Answer* in the Bass, modified so as to modulate to C♯ minor; in which key there is an *Episode* of several bars, founded on the second figure in the *Subject*, and an entry of the *Subject* in the Alto. Then follows an entry of the *Subject* in the Bass, in the original key, answered (with slight modification) in the Treble, in the key of the Dominant, then, in the original key, again, in the Alto. After a brief Episode, and one more entry in the Treble, in the original key, a *Codetta* of three bars terminates the *Fugue* of twenty-nine bars, remarkable for its compactness, simplicity, and continuity, without any special devices.

Although it is an accepted rule that, when the *Subject* begins with the *Dominant*, the *Answer* is to begin with the *Tonic*, you will find occasional instances of non-conformity to this rule, where its observance would disturb the form of the *Answer* too much. Here are some cases. (Ex. 435,

436, 437). Any attempt at a *tonal Answer* to Example 435

would be futile. A *tonal Answer* to Example 436 would destroy the *sequential* form. Example 437 might be *tonally* answered; and, later on in the *Fugue*, Bach has given the *tonal* form. Dussek, genius as he was, can hardly be cited as an authority on a matter of this kind. This *Subject* (Ex. 438) is from his *Fantasia and Fugue* dedicated to J. B. Cramer. It might be answered *tonally*, beginning with F.

An instance of another kind is furnished by the Fugue succeeding Bach's *Fantasia Cromatica*. The *Subject* commences with the *Dominant*, and the *tonal Answer* commences with the *Tonic*. Bach has, however, inserted a *passing-note*, E, between the first two notes. (Ex. 439.) A modern

editor has thought fit to alter this *Answer*, and *commence* it with E!

You will scarcely need to be reminded that the *Episodes* in a *Fugue* are very different in their nature from those in a *Rondo*. A *Fugue Episode* is not "a movement within a movement" (see p. 209), of independent origin and structure, but is a connecting link between the strictly Fugal portions of the movement, constructed from material drawn therefrom; not a break in the continuity of the movement, but only in the alternation of *Subject* and *Answer*, either for momentary relief, or to effect a progression to the harmony necessary for a Fugal entry, as I explained in the last Lecture. (See p. 325.) Some *Fugues* have but little episodical matter, being of close Fugal working throughout: *e. g.* Bach's *Das Wohltemperirte Clavier*, No. 1, which has scarcely a break to the strictly Fugal working; but, on the other hand, is rich in *Stretti*. In No. 5 there is an *Episode* of one bar between the second and third entries, in which the latter half of the first group of the *Subject* is augmented (Ex. 440); and this augmented figure is used for *Episodes* throughout, as thus (Ex. 441):

(440)

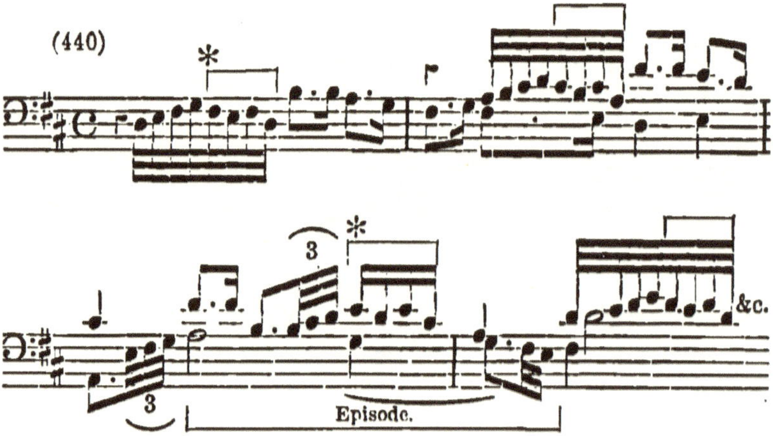

(441)

No. 12 (Ex. 442)—a *tonal Fugue*, the ascent of a 3rd in the *Answer*, for a 2nd in the *Subject* giving the 6th of the

(442)

Dominant scale to answer the 6th of the *Tonic* scale—has a beautiful sequential *Episode* between the third and fourth entries, formed from the *Counter-Subject* figure. (Ex. 443.)

(443)

This is made use of, in various superpositions, during the *Fugue:* sometimes by inverse movement, as in this passage. (Ex. 444.)

No. 21 has *Episodes* drawn from the second division of the *Subject* (Ex. 445); one being in conjunction with the first division by inverse movement. (Ex. 446.) The *Episodes* of Nos. 3, 7, 13, &c. are well worthy your special study.

Inverse movement, indicated in the Examples by ⋁, is to be observed in Nos. 6 (Ex. 447, 448), 15 (Ex. 449, 450,

451), 23 (Ex. 452, 453); this latter having only the one instance here given. This *Plagal Subject* is answered *tonally:*

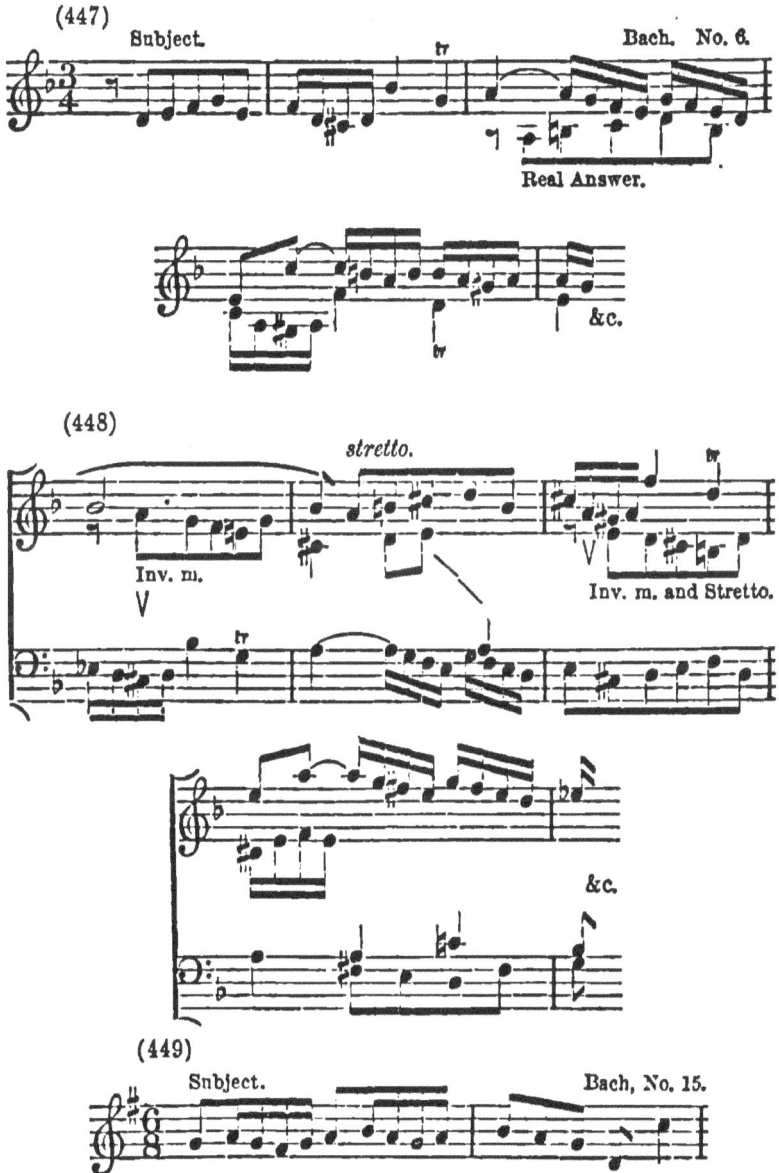

DAS WOHLTEMPERIRTE CLAVIER, NO. 23.

(453)

though it would be possible to make a *Real Answer*. In order to obtain the approach by a descent of a 5th to the *Tonic*, corresponding with that to the *Dominant*, in the *Subject*, the skip of a 3rd, instead of step of a 2nd, is made at the commencement of the Answer.

No. 20, also (Ex. 454), has instances of *Inverse movement*

(454) Subject.

&c.

Some Subjects do not bear this treatment well, sounding *ungain* when inverted. The epithet would apply in this instance, were it not for the accompanying harmonies. (Ex. 455.) Still more noticeable, in this *Fugue*, are the *Stretti*, in complete *Canon*. That at (*b*) is in the 8^{ve} below, between the upper two parts; that at (*c*) is in the 8^{ve} above, between the inner parts, the same *Stretto* as the previous one, inverted, both imitations being at the distance of half a bar. At (*d*) the *Stretto* is, similarly, between the inner parts, at half a

(455)
(*a*) Subject by Inv. mov.

bar's distance, in the 8ᵛᵉ below; but with the *Subject* by inverse movement. This is also, subsequently, inverted, in the *Fugue*. At (e) is a *Stretto* in the 5th above. These *Stretti* also appear, in the *Fugue*, with varied Contrapuntal surroundings. As the *Subject* and *Answer* run their complete length, these are *complete Stretti*.

A very close *Stretto*, inducing a *Canon* 3 in 1,—i. e. *one Antecedent*, answered successively by *two* parts, making *three* in all,—occurs in Handel's melodious *Fugue* in F♯ minor, *Suite* VI. commencing (Ex. 456). The *Canonic* passage,

which is additionally interesting by reason of the *cross accents* in the responses, proceeds thus (Ex. 457), being reduced to two parts towards the end.

XV.]   CHORUS FROM JUDAS MACCABÆUS.   359

In Handel's *Judas Maccabæus*, the Fugal *Chorus*, "*To our great God be all the honour given*," opens with *Subject* and *Counter-Subject;* the latter being the *inverse movement* form of the *Subject*, with slight modification, answering it in *Stretto*, at half a bar's distance. The *Subject*, announced by the *Soprano*, is answered *tonally* in the *Alto*, at the fourth bar. The *Counter-Subject*, announced by the *Bass*, has a *real Answer*, in the Tenor. The explanation of this is that, in the *Subject*, the *Dominant* is prominent, one of the special marks of the *Subject* of a *Tonal Fugue;* whereas, in the *Answer*, the *Dominant* scarcely appears. (Ex. 458.)

I have spoken of *entries* of the *Subject* at unexpected

intervals, or in unexpected keys. Beautiful entries and surprises are among the real points to admire in Fugues. Mendelssohn was particularly felicitous in this matter; as, indeed, in the re-introduction of the *Subject*, in his compositions generally. Some of you can confirm this by recalling the Fugues in his *Organ Sonatas*, Nos. 2 and 4. Entries should be made with the same welcomeness that I spoke of when treating of the return to the *Subject* in a *Rondo*. (See p. 256.) On the other hand, non-adepts exhibit their maladroitness very much in the awkwardness with which they bring in the *Subject*, and in the surprises that are caused by inappropriate introduction, and in fact treatment, of the *Subject*. Or else, the treatment is so similar, with so little disguise of the tautology throughout, that little interest is awakened. I have endeavoured to direct your attention to some of the interesting points, in fine examples, by great masters. These are but samples: the field is a very fruitful one. My object has been to set you thinking, and to help you to think and observe, with zest and profit: by no means to treat exhaustively of an inexhaustible subject.

LECTURE XVI.

SUMMARY OF THE DIFFERENT FORMS OF MOVEMENT, WHICH MAY SOMETIMES BLEND. EXCEPTIONAL STRUCTURES: BEETHOVEN'S SONATAS, OP. 26, OP. 54, OP. 101, OP. 27. FANTASIAS: NOT FORMLESS OR INCOHERENT. THE FANTASIAS OF MOZART, MENDELSSOHN, BENNETT, SCHUBERT, SCHUMANN, BEETHOVEN, BACH, AND THE LECTURER. THE CONCERTO. THE OVERTURE. VOCAL MUSIC. CONCLUSION.

XVI.

WE have now considered the principal forms of instrumental Movement: the *Sonata* (first Movement) structure, the *Episodical*, or *Rondo* structure, and the *Fugal*. And we have seen how these may sometimes coalesce, or run into one another. There is sometimes episodical matter in a first Movement, or Movement of *continuity* or *development*. In a *Rondo*, not only may the first portion of the Movement be like the first part of a Sonata first Movement; but, also, there may be, as one of the *Episodes*, development, working after the manner of the so-called *Free Fantasia* of a first Movement. In this case the *Episode* is not of the nature of relief from the continuity, but is integral. And, further, a *Fugue* may, in conjunction with its *fugal* structure and devices, proceed on the same lines as a first Movement, as regards order of modulation, distinct division into *first part, second part* with closer working, *return* to original key, and *Coda*, often taking the form of a *Tonic Pedal-point*. But, when all this has been said, it remains broadly true that an instrumental Movement may generally be assigned to one of these three classes or structures. Of course I am speaking of the compositions of the great Masters. And it is also true that most *Sonatas, Symphonies,* &c., commence with a *Movement of continuity,* with or without an *Introduction,* on the plan that I illustrated in the earlier Lectures. The other Movements vary in their structure, as I have said ; some *slow Movements,* and some *Finales*, being of *development* structure: others *episodical.*

There are exceptions, however. Beethoven's Sonata Op. 26 (with the *Funeral March*) commences with an *Air with Variations :* there is no Movement of *development* except the concise *Scherzo*. (See pages 290-293.) The first Movement of his Sonata Op. 54 is *episodical*. The *Sonata* Op. 101 is somewhat irregular, partaking of the *Fantasia* character, as though improvised; but by no means incoherent, inconsequential, or planless. The *Finale*, moreover, is of regular (development) structure, with *fugal* second part. And each of the two *Sonatas* Op. 27 was expressly termed by Beethoven, *Sonata quasi una Fantasia*. They are of exceptional structure, although the *Finales* are regular enough : the reminiscence of the slow Movement in that of No. 1, not interfering with the structure of the rest of the Movement, and giving effect, by contrast, to the *Presto Codetta*. Those who, like myself, contend for *design* in musical composition, and who consider that the structures sanctioned, exemplified, and developed in the works of Haydn, Mozart, Beethoven, &c., are of the highest order, and by no means effete, do not for a moment urge any servile adherence to any stereotyped form, or any repression of properly conducted experiments in the way of planning Movements; though, in counselling young writers, we do suggest as eminently reasonable, that they should perfect and prove their powers by the mastery of accepted methods, before they experimentalize, or stray into "fresh woods, and pastures new." Let not their experiments be mere erraticism, and betray the lack of real self-discipline.

The very term *Fantasia*, conjoined with that of *Sonata*, in the two instances just referred to,—Beethoven's Op. 27,—and which might have been so conjoined with some others, suggests a few remarks. Several magnificent works have borne this title : compositions by no means formless, fantastic, or erratic, but with coherence and design. The connection, however, between the several parts, portions, or Movements in some of them may be described as æsthetic or dramatic, rather than structural. Such is the case with Mozart's *Fantasia* in C minor, usually published with the

Sonata in the same key. (See p. 60.) There is a return to the opening theme which establishes the unity of the work; but there is no manifest *structural* connection between the several sections in different keys and times of which the work consists, and which lead into one another. There is no working of subjects, except by reiteration in each individual portion; and the nearest approach to completeness in any section is in the *Andante* in B♭. It is left to the hearer to sympathetically detect and follow the poetical consecution of the work as a whole.

The other *Fantasia* in the same key, C minor, by Mozart, though not without a certain character of improvisation, is regular in structure; having *second Subject* in E♭, close of first part, *second part* with modulatory working, and *recapitulation* in the usual manner.

His small Fantasia in D consists of a preludial introduction in D minor, an *Adagio*, interrupted by *Cadenza* passages, and a regularly constructed *Allegretto* with *Codetta* in D major.

His Fantasia in C major, preceding an interesting Fugue (see *Text-book*, Figs. 316, 331) is improvisatorial, but with very clear and consequential working of certain thematic figures with free modulations.

The *Fantasia*, Pianoforte Duet, to which I have referred, page 331 *et seq.*, consists of a brief *Introduction* to the *Fugue* which I have partly analysed, the *Subject* of which *Introduction* is resumed as an interruption to the *Fugue*, followed by an *Andante* of regular structure and inexpressible loveliness; and then a return to the original *Introductory* theme, and the *Fugue* with new working, which I have already described.

Mendelssohn's *Fantasia* in F♯ minor, Op. 28, was originally termed *Sonate Ecossaise*, and has, after a brief preludial passage, an *Andante* of regular structure, though of freer general character than an ordinary slow movement of a

Sonata. To this succeeds an *episodical* Movement in A major, and a *Finale* of regular continuity structure, of *Toccata* character: *i. e.* adapted to show the *touch*, the capabilities of both performer and instrument.

Sterndale Bennett's Fantasia in A, Op. 16, dedicated to Schumann, has little to distinguish it from a Sonata, except that the first Movement has no *second part* with working, returning to the *Subject* in the original key almost immediately after the close of the *first part* in the *Dominant*. Moreover, the slow Movement, *Canzonetta*, is, as its name indicates (little song), very brief, serving to introduce the *Finale* (see p. 91), which is of regular structure, with little, however, of *second part* working.

Schubert's *Fantasia* in C, Op. 15, is by no means without structural coherence, though characterized by the redundancy and structural faultiness of the Composer's instrumental works of considerable dimensions.

Schumann's *Fantasia* in C, Op. 17, develops, in a variety of ways, one initial, leading theme, as is intimated by the motto from Schlegel which is prefixed to it; partaking partly of the nature of *Variations*, and partly of continuous Movement writing.

Beethoven's *Fantasia*, Op. 77, also concludes with Variations, after some fragmentary Movements, the bearing of which upon one another is, at all events, not manifest in the way of structure or development.

There is one *Fantasia* which demands special notice: the *Fantasia Cromatica*, by Bach; characterized by Professor Macfarren as "that extraordinary anticipation of modern resources, that prophecy of all that is accomplished in the music of the present, and all that can be possible in the music of the future." * This characterization has reference to the very remarkable progressions of chromatic harmony which the work presents. The general nature of the Move-

* *Six Lectures on Harmony*, p. 179.

ment is preludial and improvisatorial, with arpeggios and scale passages on successions of harmonies, very novel in those days when the work was written; and which afford material, perhaps, for some discussion, if not controversy, even in these modern times when the nature and use of chromatic harmonies has been so systematized.

Other similar works by Bach of a *Fantasia* character might be cited. But you will understand from the references to several *Fantasias* that I have now made, that some works bearing this title have but little to distinguish them from *Sonatas;* and that others, though by no means planless, or without design, will not range themselves under either one of the forms of Movement that I have endeavoured to expound to you. I have never said that those forms are the only right forms. But, while matured genius may experimentalize and strike out new lines of thought, or courses of procedure, young writers should hardly venture in this direction, but should wait till their judgment is trained to govern and regulate their impulses.

I may mention to you that my own *Fantasia* in F minor, Op. 35, dedicated to Professor Macfarren, is regular in form, with slight deviation; consisting of a somewhat long *Introduction*, foreshadowing the *Allegro*, which is a movement of continuity, with reminiscence of the slow *Introduction* at the return to the key, and a similar reminiscence as a *Codetta*.

There is one development of the *Sonata* or, more properly, of the *Symphony* form, which I must tell you of: namely, the *Concerto*. Whereas the early form of the *Symphony* for an orchestra was termed *Concerto* (see page 4), instruments playing in *concert*, so that the term, *a Consort of Viols*, i. e. of stringed instruments, is met with (see p. 289); the occasional prominence given in some such compositions to a particular instrument, seems to have been the origin of the kind of composition which we now call a *Concerto*, in which one instrument, such as the Pianoforte, or the Violin, has an *obbligato* (obligatory, as distinguished from *ad libitum*) *Solo* part, with orchestra accompanying it; but such accompaniment not being by any means merely subordinate or *ad libitum*. The form in which the first Movement of the Pianoforte Concertos of Mozart, Beethoven, Hummel, &c., and the Violin Concertos of Beethoven, Spohr, &c., were generally written, was an enlargement of the *first Movement* form that I have already explained. There was usually a brief epitome of the Movement, announcing the principal *Subjects* by the full band; this portion being known as the *first Tutti*. This was followed by the Solo instrument, with bravura and other passages, exhibiting the capacities of the instrument; expatiating, so to speak, upon the material of that first *Tutti*, with the same order of modulations as, and, generally speaking, after the manner of a *first part*. This is termed the *first Solo*, which, however, is in conjunction with the Orchestra. Then follows a *second Tutti*, and a *second Solo*, working the material of the first part. Then the return to the key and Subject by a brief *third Tutti*, followed by a *third Solo;* these constituting the *Recapitulation.* Towards the end of the Movement it was usual to have a *pause* on a $\tfrac{6}{4}$ chord; and, at this point the performer played a *Cadenza*, supposed to be an improvisation upon some of the material of the Movement. This form has been in more recent times considerably modified and abridged; the Solo instrument and the orchestra amalgamating more, curtailing the *Tuttis*. This is exemplified in the Pianoforte Concertos of Mendelssohn, &c. The Slow Movements of Concertos have varied in form. For the last Movement, the *Rondo* form is frequently chosen. Works of the same class have also been written more after the manner of a *Fantasia ;* such as the *Concert-Stück* by Weber.

The *Overture*, or orchestral prelude to an *Oratorio* or

Opera, has varied at different times, and still varies in form. In early times it sometimes consisted of a *series of Movements*, including a *Fugue*, or a dance-movement, as in the case of Handel's Overture to "*Samson*," which has both *Fugue* and *Minuet*. The Overture to "*The Messiah*" consists simply of an *Introduction* and *Fugue*. Some *Overtures* are on the same plan as a first Movement; either, as in Mozart's "*Figaro*," without a second part, or *Free Fantasia*; or with such working as in his "*Don Giovanni*." His "*Zauberflöte*" Overture is a marvellous union of the *Fugal* and *first Movement* forms. It has been called "the despair of Overture writers." The *Overture* to Mendelssohn's "*Elijah*" is *fugal*. Some *Overtures* are essentially dramatic, taking their character, and even their form, from the drama which they precede. Weber's "*Der Freischütz*" and "*Euryanthe*" may be cited as examples. Some, such perhaps as his "*Preciosa*," may be termed melodramatic: though this epithet would be more applicable to certain Overtures by inferior composers.

An interesting method of presenting the same idea or theme in different aspects or forms, is furnished by *Variations* on an *Air* or *Melody*: a harmonized Melody, that is. This may call into use the various harmonic and contrapuntal resources of Music, and evince the insight of the Composer into the suggestiveness of simple themes. In old times, *Double* was the term used for that which we call a *Variation*. In those *Doubles* to be found in the *Suites* by early English and French composers, such as William Byrd, Dr. John Bull, Dr. John Blow, Rameau, Couperin, &c., little more is done than to decorate the melody and harmony by *Arpeggios*, *Scales*, and the like; such decorative passages being termed *Divisions*. The outline remained, both of melody and harmony. Sometimes such *Variations* were upon a *Ground Bass*: the same Bass, with or without embellishment, repeated any number of times. Examples are furnished by

Handel's *Passecaille* in G minor, with 13 Variations: his *Chaconne* in G major, with 61 Variations, &c. In more modern times the tendency has often been rather to disguise than to ornament the original theme. *Variations* may present different *harmonious* treatment of the same *melody;* different *melodious* treatment of the same *harmony;* *contrapuntal* involvements, such as are exemplified in Bach's 30 *Variations* in G, with *Canons* in all the intervals, a *Fughetta*, &c.; *rhythmical* changes, and various devices within reach of the trained Musician. Tawdry *Variations*, written merely for the display of executive skill, have abounded; but the great masters have brought the resources of their knowledge and skill to bear upon the production of Variations of much musical interest.

Vocal Music is, of course, influenced in its forms by the words, and constitutes a wide subject for analysis. But many *Choruses* in *Oratorios*, and similar works, are, in the main, constructed very much on the same plan as a *first Movement*: others are *fugal*. I have confined my analyses made in your hearing mainly to instrumental works.

Remember that, while a true work of Art has *design, plan, development*, all of which may be analysed, there remains underlying all, permeating all, that subtle sentiment, the offspring of genius, which can neither be defined nor analysed. By training, and such explanations as I have endeavoured to furnish you with, you may learn how to analyse, and, therefore, intelligently to understand and enjoy great Music. But the subtle essence appeals to your sensibilities, which may be kindled, awakened, regulated,—but not imparted. All expositions will avail little unless there is, in yourselves, the sympathetic faculty to appreciate and enjoy the sublime or the beautiful.

INDEX.

Accent, Cross 187	No. 21 349
Alternativo 290	,, 23 350
Analysis defined 3	,, 31 338
Answer, Fugue, Real and	,, 41 341
Tonal 305, 316	*Fantasia Cromatica* ... 366
Answer, Exceptional 345	Fugue of ditto 345
Antecedent 152, 155	Fugue in A 346
Arsin et Thesin, Per 189	,, ,, C minor (2 part) 320
Attendant Keys ... 149, *et seq.*	,, ,, C minor (3 part) 346
Augmentation, 133, 153, 176, 348	,, ,, D minor 322, *et seq.*
Authentic Mode and Fugue	,, ,, E minor 345
Subject 316	*Partita* No. 2. (Rondeau) 223
	Scherzo in A minor (Partita
Bach, Joh. Seb., Art of Fugue 342	No. 3) 290
Das Wohltemperirte Clavier	*Suites Françaises* Nos. 5, 6 16
(48 Preludes and Fugues):—	30 Variations 370
No. 1 342	Banister, H. C., *Allegretto*
,, 2 327	*alla Marcia* 268
,, 3 349	Fantasia, Op. 35 367
,, 4 ... ... 314, 342	Beethoven, Andante, Op. 35 105
,, 5 ... ... 341, 348	Fantasia, Op. 77 366
,, 6 ... ... 327, 350	Overture to *Leonora* ... 50
,, 7 349	Quartet, Op. 18, No. 1 ... 304
,, 8 327	,, ,, ,, ,, 4 87, 305
,, 9 ... ... 343, *et seq.*	Quintet, Op. 4 267
,, 10 320	,, ,, 29 ... 51, 200-1
,, 12 ... ... 348, *et seq.*	Rondos, Op. 51 266
,, 13 349	Septet, Op. 20 ... 202, *et seq.*
,, 14 327	Sestet, Op. 81 267
,, 15 351	Sonatas (Solo):—
,, 16 ... ... 315, 321	Op. 2, No. 1 60, 76, 130, 166,
,, 17 341	208, 278, 293
,, 20 354	,, ,, ,, 2 41, 163, 261, 278

Beethoven, Sonatas, *continued*—
Op. 2, No. 3   43, 165, 280, 294
Op. 7   140, 142, 258, 276, 281
Op. 10, No. 1 ... ...   62, 278
,, ,, ,, 2 ... 8, 26, 79, 120
,, ,, ,, 3   292
Op. 13   ...   71, 93, 97-9, 214
Op. 14, No. 1 ...   20, 85, 119,
                                208, 292
Op. 14, No. 2   277
Op. 22   27, 160, 176, 261, 278,
                                    292
Op. 26   ... ...   261, 292 363
Op. 27, Nos. 1, 2   364
,, ,, No. 2 ... ...   75, 292
Op. 28   ...   11, 179, 216, 262
Op. 31, No. 1 ...   47, 86, 264
,, ,, ,, 2   73, 274, *et seq.*
,, ,, ,, 3   11, 22, 81, 85,
        142, 274, 275, 290, 292
Op. 49. No. 1 ...   64, 123, 278
,, ,, ,, 2 ... ...   11, 17
Op. 53   ... ...   48, 86, 105
Op. 54   364
Op. 57   ...   65, 75, 89, 283
Op. 79   216
Op. 81*a* 101, 142
Op. 90   76
Op. 101   ... ...   310, 364
Op. 106   ... ...   49, 78, 181
Op. 111   ...   77, 99, 165, *et seq.*
Sonatas, Pianoforte and
  Violin, Op. 12, No. 2 ...   47
            Op. 23, ,, 1 ...   77
            Op. 30   ,, 2 ...   310
            ,, ,,   ,, 3 ...   47
            Op. 47   94
Symphonies :—
No. 1   306
,, 4   110
,, 5   89
,, 7   108
,, 9   89
Trio (Pianoforte & strings),
  Op. 97   51
Trio (strings), Op. 9   ...   267
Bennett (W. Sterndale), Fantasia, Op. 16   ...   91, 366

Romance, Op. 14, No. 3   91
Rondeau à la Polonaise   218,
                                267
Rondo Piacevole, Op. 25   267
Sonata, Op. 13   91
Binary form   130
Cadence, Imperfect 6, 11
Cadence, Interrupted, Examples of   52, 124, 155, 163,
                        164, 280, 281
Cadence, Inverted   9
,, Plagal (Coda)   273, &c.
Cadenza (or Cadence) in Concerto   368
Canon 132, 152, 218, 265, 306-309
,, (in Stretto)   318
,, 3 in 1   358
Cantata   4
Chamber Music   200
Chopin   3
Clementi, Sonata, Op. 40,
  No. 1., Canon from   ...   308
Coda   ... ...   5, 273, *et seq.*
  Examples from Mozart 200,
                    243, 244, 248, 283
Codetta   176, 212, 216, 273, 274,
                                    284
Concertante 184, 201
Concerted music 183, 200
Concerto 4, 289, 367
Consequent 152, 155
Continuity, Movement of ...   4
Contrapuntal devices   305
Contrary Motion   153
Counter-exposition   341
Counterpoint, Double 133, 179, 317
,, ,, Quintuple ...   283
Counter-subject   317
Couperin, Rondeaux by 219, *et seq.*

Dance-measures   289
Development   ...   5, 117, 203
,, ,,   Movement of ...   4
Diminution   ...   133, 153, 187
Dominant, Second Subject in   15
Double Dominant   41
Duplex form   130

INDEX.

Dussek 3, 257
  Consolation, La ... 257, 267
  Elegy Sonata 257
  Fantasia and Fugue in F
    minor 346
  Sonata, Op. 35, No. 2 151, 256
    ,, Op. 44 (*Farewell*)
      107, 257
  ,, Op. 75 ,, 257
  ,, Op. 77 (*L'Invoca-*
    tion) 257, 307

Enharmonic change 98, 99, 126,
    127, 140, 262
Enharmonic notation ... 186
  ,, Implied 43, 50, 260, 261
  ,, Modulation 129, 139,
    142, 146, 147, 165, 335
Entries in Fugue 359
Episode (in Movement) 207, 208, 229
  ,, in Fugue 317, 329, 347
  ,, (Trio of Minuet) ... 290
Episodes, Movements with
    two ... ... 218, &c.
Exposition 318
  ,, Counter- 341

False Relation, apparent ... 111
Fantasia 364
Fantasia, Free ... 5, 117, 118, 137, *et seq.*
Figured Basses 10, 129, 238, 280
Figures, Working of 12, 133, 144,
    153, 171, 177, 179, 280
Fugue ... ... 313, *et seq.*
  Unexpected Entries in 330, 336, 337, 341, 359
  Exceptional Answers in 345, *et seq.*
  How to analyze 319

Genius and mastery compared 3
Grammatical infringements
  by great Composers 113, 134, 257

Handel Chaconne with varia-
  tions 370
  Fugue in B minor 337
  Fugue in F♯ minor 358
  Judas Maccabæus, Fugue
    from 359
  Messiah, Overture 369
  Suite No. 2 16
  Passecaille with varia-
    tions 370
  Messiah, "*And With His
    Stripes*" from 315
Haydn 130
  Master of Rhythm 305
  Minuets 290, 303
  Quartets 305
  ,, in C 233
  ,, in D (*a*) 233
  ,, ,, (*b*) 301
  ,, in D minor (*a*) 187
  ,, in ,, ,, (*b*) 306
  ,, in E♭ 184, *et seq.*
  ,, in G 303
  Sonatas, No. 5 (Pauer's
    Edition) in C... ... 28, 232
  Sonatas, No. 6 in G ... 232
  ,, ,, 7 in E ... 291
  ,, ,, 10 in F ... 232
  ,, ,, 12 in D ... 232
  ,, ,, 13 in B minor 54, 82, 91, 127, 156
  ,, ,, 17 in D ... 158
  ,, ,, 19 in G ... 232
  ,, ,, 20 in D ... 231
  ,, ,, 23 in G minor 56, 82, 91, 143, 144
  ,, ,, 24 in C ... 229
  ,, ,, 25 in E ... 124
  ,, ,, 27 in C minor 57
  ,, ,, 28 in A♭ 10, 81
  ,, ,, 29 in E♭ ... 30
  ,, ,, 30 in D 6, 171, 232
  ,, ,, 31 in C♯ minor 57, 138
  ,, ,, 32 in E♭ 31, 173, 210
  ,, ,, 33 in E minor 91

INDEX.

Haydn's Sonata, No. 34 in E♭ 138, 210, 273
Higgs, *Fugue Primer* ... 317, 320
Hummel 3

Imitation ... 152, 153, 181, 182
Canonical 265
Imitational Structure and workings, 46, 133, 153, 158, 159, 160, 161, 165, 190-193, 198, 262, 294, 295
Intermezzo 212, 310
Introduction to Movements 97, *et seq.*
Inverse Movement 133, 152, 187, 198, 335, 349-352
Inversion of parts 171, 172, 174, 283

Macfarren, G. A., Vocal Rondo 218
„ „ quoted ... 306
„ on Bach's *Fantasia Cromatica* 366
Mastery of resources 3
Mediant, Second Subject in 55, *et seq.*, 151
Mendelssohn, Athalie March 268
Elijah, Overture 369
Fantasia in F♯ minor, Op. 28 365
Fugues, Op. 35, Nos. 2, 6 315
Fugue (Organ), Op. 37, No. 3 342
Organ Sonatas, Nos. 2, 4 360
Perpetuum Mobile 267
Rivulet, Op. 16 267
Scherzi 290
Symphony (Scotch) 76, 108, 283
Song without words, Book I. No. 5 90
Minuet 137, 289
Haydn's extension of ... 290
Second (or Trio) 290
Structure of 292
Minor Mode, Character of 71
Modes, Authentic and Plagal 316
Modification of Subject commencement in Fugue ... 338
Modulation 129, 130, 137, 143, 147, 151, 165, 174

Motivi 12
Motivo 263
Movement, Defined 3
„ „ of continuity or development ... 4, 219
Episodical 4, 207, 209, 219, 229, 232
Exceptional structure ... 363
Different forms 268
Sometimes coalesce 363
Movements, Slow ... 137, 210
Order of 137
Mozart, Duet in F ... 182, 250
Fantasia & Fugue (Pianoforte Duet) in F minor 331, 341
Minuet in D 295
„ in *Don Giovanni* 290
Non temer 218
Overtures, *Don Giovanni* ⎫
„ *Figaro* ... ⎬ 369
„ *Zauberflöte* ⎭
Quartets, No. 1 315
„ „ 2 189
„ „ 4 ... 191, 208
„ „ 5 193
„ „ 6 110
„ „ 9 198
„ „ 10 303
Quintets, No. 1 308
„ „ 3 ... 144, 200
Rondos (so-called) in B♭ and D 219
Rondo in A minor 247
Sonatas, No. 1 (Pauer's Edition) in C 173
Sonatas, No. 2 in F ... 33
„ „ 3 in B♭ ... 235
„ „ 5 in G 7, 119, 276
„ „ 6 in D ... 239
„ „ 7 in C 19, 234, 276-7
„ „ 8 in A minor 59, 82, 91, 124, 239
„ „ 9 in D 122, 237
„ „ 10 in C 211, 277
„ „ 11 in A 238, 278

INDEX.   375

Mozart's Sonatas, *continued*—
Sonatas, No. 12 in F ... 119
  ,,   ,, 14 in C minor 60, 84, 128, 212, 239, 279, 291
  ,, No. 15 in F 153, 156, 242
  ,,   ,, 16 in C 18, 79, 121
  ,,   ,, 17 in F ... 119
  ,,   ,, 18 in B♭ ... 35
  ,,   ,, 19 in D 213, 245
Symphonies (*Breitkopf and Härtel*), No. 36 in C ... 86
Symphonies, No. 39 in E♭ 140, 141
  ,,   ,, 40 in G minor 92, 145, 150
Symphonies, No. 41 in C (*Jupiter*) 283, 315

Nocturnes 209
Notation, Enharmonic ... 215
False instances of 66, 100, 126, 282, 283

Overture 369

Partita 15, 289
Pedal-Bass 222, 247, 265, 273, 279
Pedal-point 319
Phrase 7
Plagal Mode 316
  ,, Cadence 273, 274
Prout, Symphony in F 26, 27

Quartets (see Beethoven, Haydn, Mozart) 184
Quintuple Counterpoint ... 283

Rameau, Tambourin or Rondo by 222
Real answer 305, 316
Recapitulation (in Movement) 5, 78, *et seq.*
Relative Keys ... 149, *et seq.*
Retrograde motion 153
Return to Subject 5, 256, 261
Rhythm 7, 45, 134
  ,, 3 bar 167
  ,, 5 bar 171, 303

Rhythm, 6 bar 176, 182, 183, 229
  ,, broken 134, 303
  ,, overlapping 304
Rhythmical devices 293, 297-301
Rondel, Roundel, Roundelay 218
Rondo, Rondeau, Rondino, Rondoletto 218, 255
Term misapplied 219, 232, 267
Some Rondos not so-called 218
  ,, Vocal 218
Round 218
Roundels by Mr. Swinburne 203, 256

Scherzo 137, 290, 292
Schumann, Sonata, Op. 22 91
Second Part 5, 117, 118, 137, 172
Section 7
Sonata (or First Movement) form 4
Sonatina 5
Spohr, Quartets 184
  ,, Nonet 202
Stretto 155, 177, 279, 318
Subject 4
Divisions of 7
Episodical 119
First 5
Second 5, 15, 18, 41
In exceptional keys ... 43, 151
In Mediant 55
In Minor key ... 54, 71, *et seq.*
In new aspects 117
Fugue and Sonata compared 314
Suite 15, 289
Superpositions in Fugue ... 325
Swinburne, Roundels by 203, 256
Symphony 4, 289
Syncopation 167

Tambourin 222
Tonal 305, 316
Transition 15
Trinary 218
Trio (of Minuet, &c.) 290
Triplex 218

Valse 209

Variations	369
Weber, *Il Moto continuo* ...	267
Polonaises (Polaccas) ...	218
Sonata, Op. 49	91
,, Op. 70	91
Overtures	369
Working (see *Development*)	5, 117, 131, 203
Canonical	265
Contrapuntal	133, 173, 262, 305
Fragmentary	293
Fugal,	160, 181, 183, 234, 305, 306

THE END.

Richard Clay & Sons, Limited, London & Bungay.

By the same Author.

TEXT-BOOK OF MUSIC. Thirteenth Edition. 30th Thousand. With Emendations and Additions. Fcap. 8vo. cloth. Price 5s.

This Manual contains chapters on Notation, Harmony, and Counterpoint; Modulation, Rhythm, Canon, Fugue, Voices, and Instruments; together with Exercises on Harmony, an Appendix of Examination Papers, and a copious Index and Glossary of Musical Terms.

". . . . We are bound to accord the highest praise to the work, which is so logically arranged throughout that reference to any special portion of it can be readily made. . . . We have a remarkably clear exposition of notation, time, accent, and other elementary matters unfortunately too often passed over by students. Especially must we praise the author's explanation of the difference between Simple and Compound Time, the widely-spread ignorance of which subject causes half the false emphasis we are compelled to listen to amongst amateurs."—*Musical Times*, April, 1873.

"A capital little work on the theory of music."—*Athenæum*, August 4, 1883.

"Mr. H. C. Banister's book on 'Music,' which is one of the best and most trustworthy I know."—Mr. E. Prout in *The Academy*, March 16, 1878.

"Banister's 'Music' still keeps, as it deserves, a prominent place in the estimation of students and teachers."—*The Monthly Musical Record*, April 1, 1884.

". . . . A volume which is remarkable for the amount of information comprised in so small a compass. The book is divided into three principal parts, each of which is sub-divided into chapters which treat of the various details associated with the general subjects of notation, musical theory, and practical composition. All this wide field is amply surveyed, and valuable information succinctly and clearly imparted, with occasional illustrative musical quotations from classical works. . . ."—*Daily News*.

"The thoroughness of the manual, the clear and happy language he employs, and the soundness of his doctrines, render it one of the most useful treatises on the art of music we have ever seen."—*Musical Standard*.

". . . . The neat, clear, and concise language in which it is written makes it a refreshing and agreeable study for musical students. The fact that an eleventh edition has been called for is a sufficient witness to its importance and widespread popularity among musicians."—From the *Biographical Dictionary of Musicians*, by JAMES D. BROWN, Glasgow, 1886.

LONDON:
GEORGE BELL AND SONS, YORK STREET, COVENT GARDEN.

Second Edition with an additional Paper.

MUSICAL ART AND STUDY:
PAPERS FOR MUSICIANS.

Printed on Handmade Paper. Foolscap 8vo, cloth, 2s.

No. I.—OUR ART AND OUR PROFESSION. (*Read before the National Society of Professional Musicians.*) No. II.—SOME METHODS OF MUSICAL STUDY. (*Read before the North-East London Society of Musicians.*) No. III.—SOME MUSICAL ETHICS AND ANALOGIES. (*Read before the College of Organists.*) No. IV.—THE ENJOYMENT OF MUSIC. (*Read before the College of Organists, June 28, 1887.*)

OPINIONS OF THE PRESS.

"THE volume contains three papers, ... all of which exhibit a commendable desire to elevate the art in public estimation, and a keen perception as to the best method of effecting this object. We cordially commend both Mr. Banister's works as most valuable aids to the true appreciation of the imperishable creations of musical art."—*Musical Times*, August 1, 1887.

"The book is full of material for thought, and should be widely read."—*Musical Standard*, October 27, 1887.

"The essays here given . . . . give evidence of a happy union of general culture with musical knowledge—a union made especially apparent, and with happy effect, in the last of the three, dealing with certain peculiarities possessed in common by music with other arts, and even with certain moral qualities. . . . For the rest, acknowledgment should not be omitted of the useful hints and suggestive remarks to be found in these lectures, and of the high views advanced by their author regarding the mission and possibilities of music. . . ."—*Musical World*, July 7, 1887.

"These delightful 'papers for musicians' . . . were delivered to different audiences. . . . We can, however, well believe that those who heard them would be desirous to see them in a collected and permanent form. The *obiter dicta* of Professor Banister on musical topics are, indeed, well worth preserving, and it is to men of a kindred spirit with the writer of these essays that the musical profession must look if it would be saved from narrow and bigoted views of music as an art. . . . As an example of the happy manner and delightful style in which these thoughtful and suggestive papers are written, we will quote the following remarks upon those whose due appreciation of music is narrowed by want of musical knowledge. . . . To the learned contrapuntist who has become the slave of his art, and the musical amateur who is technically unlearned, these papers appeal alike, while to the general reader they will be welcome because of their general literary merits and 'words that glow and thoughts that speak.'"—*Musical Society*, October 1, 1887.

"Good thoughts neatly expressed."—*Academy*, September 3, 1887.

"They all well repay reading, but for teachers and students the second will have most interest. It contains some valuable hints on the study of music, which is unfortunately still too often pursued on the most irrational principles, and rendered by the teacher the most uninteresting subject in the school curriculum."—*Journal of Education*, October 1, 1887.

Ninth Edition, 17th thousand, revised to date (1888), *fcp. 8vo, 3s. 6d.*

A CONCISE HISTORY OF MUSIC

FROM THE COMMENCEMENT OF THE CHRISTIAN ERA TO THE PRESENT TIME. FOR THE USE OF STUDENTS.

BY THE

Rev. H. G. BONAVIA HUNT, Mus. Doc., F.R.S.E.,
Warden of Trinity College, London; late Lecturer on Musical History in the same College. Honorary Fellow of the Philharmonic Society of London.

"Mr. Hunt has produced a well-arranged and really concise history of the subject with which he deals. The student 'is warned' in the preface 'that he is not to expect what is called a readable book,' but we feel bound to say that Mr. Hunt's work is, in the proper sense of the word, far more readable than books which attempt to combine valuable information with attractiveness by tricks to which Mr. Hunt has not condescended."—*Saturday Review.*

"Mr. Hunt has the enviable power of giving much information in few words; he has, therefore, in this small volume afforded valuable assistance to musical students preparing for competitive examinations, which they could not so easily obtain elsewhere."—*Musical Standard.*

Small Post 8vo, 3s. 6d.

SCHUMANN: His Life and Works. By A. Reissmann. Translated from the third German edition by A. L. Alger.

"Herr Reissmann's *Life of Schumann* stands very high among the biographies of the masters. The translator has done his work, on the whole, with very great skill."—*Musical World.*

"As a concise guide to Schumann's musical works we do not know a more convenient little volume."—*Saturday Review.*

Crown 8vo, 7s. 6d.

SCHUMANN'S EARLY LETTERS. Originally published by his wife. Translated by May Herbert. With a Preface by Sir George Grove, D.C.L.

"A fascinating little volume."—*Athenæum.*

Small Post 8vo, 3s. 6d.

HOFFMANN'S WORKS. The Serapion Brethren. Translated from the German by Major Alex. Ewing. Vol. I. containing Thirteen Tales. Vol. II. *in the press.*

"Hoffmann's observations on musical subjects are, perhaps, of the most abiding interest: at times he seems to be thinking in music and at a loss for words to express his thoughts."—*St. James's Gazette.*

LONDON:
GEORGE BELL AND SONS, YORK STREET, COVENT GARDEN.

November 1889.

A CLASSIFIED LIST
OF
EDUCATIONAL WORKS
PUBLISHED BY
GEORGE BELL & SONS.

Cambridge Calendar. Published Annually (*August*). 6s. 6d.
Student's Guide to the University of Cambridge. 6s. 6d.
Oxford : Its Life and Schools. 7s. 6d.
The Schoolmaster's Calendar. Published Annually (*December*). 1s.

BIBLIOTHECA CLASSICA.

A Series of Greek and Latin Authors, with English Notes, edited by eminent Scholars. 8vo.

*** *The Works with an asterisk* (*) *prefixed can only be had in the Sets of 26 Vols.*

Aeschylus. By F. A. Paley, M.A., LL.D. 8s.
Cicero's Orations. By G. Long, M.A. 4 vols. 32s.
Demosthenes. By R. Whiston, M.A. 2 vols. 10s.
Euripides. By F. A. Paley, M.A., LL.D. 3 vols. 24s.
Homer. By F. A. Paley, M.A., LL.D. The Iliad, 2 vols. 14s.
Herodotus. By Rev. J. W. Blakesley, B.D. 2 vols. 12s.
Hesiod. By F. A. Paley, M.A., LL.D. 5s.
Horace. By Rev. A. J. Macleane, M.A. 8s.
Juvenal and Persius. By Rev. A. J. Macleane, M.A. 6s.
Plato. By W. H. Thompson, D.D. 2 vols. 5s. each.
Sophocles. Vol. I. By Rev. F. H. Blaydes, M.A. 8s.
——— Vol. II. F. A. Paley, M.A., LL.D. 6s.
*Tacitus: The Annals. By the Rev. P. Frost. 8s.
*Terence. By E. St. J. Parry, M.A. 8s.
Virgil. By J. Conington, M.A. Revised by Professor H. Nettleship.
3 vols. 10s. 6d. each.
An Atlas of Classical Geography; 24 Maps with coloured Outlines. Imp. 8vo. 6s.

GRAMMAR-SCHOOL CLASSICS.

A Series of Greek and Latin Authors, with English Notes.
Fcap. 8vo.

Cæsar: De Bello Gallico. By George Long, M.A. 4s.
—— Books I.-III. For Junior Classes. By G. Long, M.A. 1s. 6d.
—— Books IV. and V. 1s. 6d. Books VI. and VII. 1s. 6d.

Catullus, Tibullus, and Propertius. Selected Poems. With Life. By Rev. A. H. Wratislaw. 2s. 6d.

Cicero: De Senectute, De Amicitia, and Select Epistles. By George Long, M.A. 3s.

Cornelius Nepos. By Rev. J. F. Macmichael. 2s.

Homer: Iliad. Books I.-XII. By F. A. Paley, M.A., LL.D. 4s. 6d. Also in 2 parts, 2s. 6d. each.

Horace: With Life. By A. J. Macleane, M.A. 3s. 6d. In 2 parts, 2s. each.

Juvenal: Sixteen Satires. By H. Prior, M.A. 3s. 6d.

Martial: Select Epigrams. With Life. By F. A. Paley, M.A., LL.D. 4s. 6d.

Ovid: the Fasti. By F. A. Paley, M.A., LL.D. 3s. 6d. Books I. and II. 1s. 6d. Books III. and IV. 1s. 6d.

Sallust: Catilina and Jugurtha. With Life. By G. Long, M.A. and J. G. Frazer. 3s. 6d., or separately, 2s. each.

Tacitus: Germania and Agricola. By Rev. P. Frost. 2s. 6d.

Virgil: Bucolics, Georgics, and Æneid, Books I.-IV. Abridged from Professor Conington's Edition. 4s. 6d.—Æneid, Books V.-XII. 4s. 6d. Also in 9 separate Volumes, as follows, 1s. 6d. each:—Bucolics—Georgics, I. and II.—Georgics, III. and IV.—Æneid, I. and II.—Æneid, III. and IV.—Æneid, V. and VI.—Æneid, VII. and VIII.—Æneid, IX. and X.—Æneid, XI. and XII.

Xenophon: The Anabasis. With Life. By Rev. J. F. Macmichael. 3s. 6d. Also in 4 separate volumes, 1s. 6d. each:—Book I. (with Life, Introduction, Itinerary, and Three Maps)—Books II. and III.—IV. and V.—VI. and VII.

—— The Cyropædia. By G. M. Gorham, M.A. 3s. 6d. Books I. and II. 1s. 6d.—Books V. and VI. 1s. 6d.

—— Memorabilia. By Percival Frost, M.A. 3s.

A Grammar-School Atlas of Classical Geography, containing Ten selected Maps. Imperial 8vo. 3s.

Uniform with the Series.

The New Testament, in Greek. With English Notes, &c. By Rev. J. F. Macmichael. 4s. 6d. In 5 parts, The Four Gospels and the Acts. Sewed, 6d. each.

Educational Works. 3

CAMBRIDGE GREEK AND LATIN TEXTS.

Aeschylus. By F. A. Paley, M.A., LL.D. 2s.
Cæsar: De Bello Gallico. By G. Long, M.A. 1s. 6d.
Cicero: De Senectute et De Amicitia, et Epistolæ Selectæ. By G. Long, M.A. 1s. 6d.
Ciceronis Orationes. In Verrem. By G. Long, M.A. 2s. 6d.
Euripides. By F. A. Paley, M.A., LL.D. 3 vols. 2s. each.
Herodotus. By J. G. Blakesley, B.D. 2 vols. 5s.
Homeri Ilias. I.-XII. By F. A. Paley, M.A., LL.D. 1s. 6d.
Horatius. By A. J. Macleane, M.A. 1s. 6d.
Juvenal et Persius. By A. J. Macleane, M.A. 1s. 6d.
Lucretius. By H. A. J. Munro, M.A. 2s.
Sallusti Crispi Catilina et Jugurtha. By G. Long, M.A. 1s. 6d.
Sophocles. By F. A. Paley, M.A., LL.D. 2s. 6d.
Terenti Comœdiæ. By W. Wagner, Ph.D. 2s.
Thucydides. By J. G. Donaldson, D.D. 2 vols. 4s.
Virgilius. By J. Conington, M.A. 2s.
Xenophontis Expeditio Cyri. By J. F. Macmichael, B.A. 1s. 6d.
Novum Testamentum Græce. By F. H. Scrivener, M.A., D.C.L. 4s. 6d. An edition with wide margin for notes, half bound, 12s. EDITIO MAJOR, with additional Readings and References. 7s. 6d. *See page* 14.

CAMBRIDGE TEXTS WITH NOTES.

A Selection of the most usually read of the Greek and Latin Authors, Annotated for Schools. Edited by well-known Classical Scholars. Fcap. 8vo. 1s. 6d. each, with exceptions.

'Dr. Paley's vast learning and keen appreciation of the difficulties of beginners make his school editions as valuable as they are popular. In many respects he sets a brilliant example to younger scholars.'—*Athenæum.*

'We hold in high value these handy Cambridge texts with Notes.'—*Saturday Review.*

Aeschylus. Prometheus Vinctus.—Septem contra Thebas.—Agamemnon.—Persae.—Eumenides.—Choephoroe. By F.A. Paley, M.A., LL.D.
Euripides. Alcestis.—Medea.—Hippolytus.—Hecuba.—Bacchae. —Ion. 2s.—Orestes. — Phoenissae.—Troades.—Hercules Furens.—Andromache.—Iphigenia in Tauris.—Supplices. By F. A. Paley, M.A., LL.D.
Homer. Iliad. Book I. By F. A. Paley, M.A., LL.D. 1s.
Sophocles. Oedipus Tyrannus.—Oedipus Coloneus.—Antigone. —Electra—Ajax. By F. A. Paley, M.A., LL.D.
Xenophon. Anabasis. In 6 vols. By J. E. Melhuish, M.A., Assistant Classical Master at St. Paul's School.
——— Hellenics, Book II. By L. D. Dowdall, M.A., B.D. 2s.
——— Hellenics. Book I. By L. D. Dowdall, M.A., B.D.
[*In the press.*
Cicero. De Senectute, De Amicitia and Epistolæ Selectæ. By G. Long, M.A.
Ovid. Fasti. By F. A. Paley, M.A LL.D. In 3 vols., 2 books in each. 2s. each vol.

Ovid. Selections. Amores, Tristia, Heroides, Metamorphoses.
By A. J. Macleane, M.A.
Terence. Andria.—Hauton Timorumenos.—Phormio.—Adelphoe.
By Professor Wagner, Ph.D.
Virgil. Professor Conington's edition, abridged in 12 vols.
Others in preparation.

PUBLIC SCHOOL SERIES.
A Series of Classical Texts, annotated by well-known Scholars. Cr. 8vo.

Aristophanes. The Peace. By F. A. Paley, M.A., LL.D. 4s. 6d.
—— The Acharnians. By F. A. Paley, M.A., LL.D. 4s. 6d.
—— The Frogs. By F. A. Paley, M.A., LL.D. 4s. 6d.
Cicero. The Letters to Atticus. Bk. I. By A. Pretor, M.A. 4s. 6d.
Demosthenes de Falsa Legatione. By R. Shilleto, M.A. 6s.
—— The Law of Leptines. By B. W. Beatson, M.A. 3s. 6d.
Livy. Book XXI. Edited, with Introduction, Notes, and Maps, by the Rev. L. D. Dowdall, M.A., B.D. 3s. 6d.
—— Book XXII. Edited, &c., by Rev. L. D. Dowdall, M.A., B.D. 3s. 6d.
Plato. The Apology of Socrates and Crito. By W. Wagner, Ph.D. 10th Edition. 3s. 6d. Cheap Edition, limp cloth, 2s. 6d.
—— The Phædo. 9th Edition. By W. Wagner, Ph.D. 5s. 6d.
—— The Protagoras. 4th Edition. By W. Wayte, M.A. 4s. 6d.
—— The Euthyphro. 3rd Edition. By G. H. Wells, M.A. 3s.
—— The Euthydemus. By G. H. Wells, M.A. 4s.
—— The Republic. Books I. & II. By G. H. Wells, M.A. 3rd Edition. 5s. 6d.
Plautus. The Aulularia. By W. Wagner, Ph.D. 3rd Edition. 4s. 6d.
—— The Trinummus. By W. Wagner, Ph.D. 3rd Edition. 4s. 6d.
—— The Menaechmei. By W. Wagner, Ph.D. 2nd Edit. 4s. 6d.
—— The Mostellaria. By Prof. E. A. Sonnenschein. 5s.
—— The Rudens. Edited by Prof. E. A. Sonnenschein.
[*In the press.*
Sophocles. The Trachiniæ. By A. Pretor, M.A. 4s. 6d.
Sophocles. The Oedipus Tyrannus. By B. H. Kennedy, D.D. 5s.
Terence. By W. Wagner, Ph.D. 2nd Edition. 7s. 6d.
Theocritus. By F. A. Paley, M.A., LL.D. 2nd Edition. 4s. 6d.
Thucydides. Book VI. By T. W. Dougan, M.A., Fellow of St. John's College, Cambridge. 3s. 6d.
Others in preparation.

CRITICAL AND ANNOTATED EDITIONS.
Aristophanis Comœdiæ. By H. A. Holden, LL.D. 8vo. 2 vols. Notes, Illustrations, and Maps. 23s. 6d. Plays sold separately.
Cæsar's Seventh Campaign in Gaul, B.C. 52. By Rev. W. C. Compton, M.A., Assistant Master, Uppingham School. Crown 8vo. 4s.

Educational Works. 5

Calpurnius Siculus. By C. H. Keene, M.A. Crown 8vo. 6s.
Catullus. A New Text, with Critical Notes and Introduction by Dr. J. P. Postgate. Japanese vellum. Foolscap 8vo. 3s.
Corpus Poetarum Latinorum. Edited by Walker. 1 vol. 8vo. 18s.
Horace. Quinti Horatii Flacci Opera. By H. A. J. Munro, M.A. Large 8vo. 10s. 6d.
Livy. The first five Books. By J. Prendeville. 12mo. roan, 5s. Or Books I.-III. 3s. 6d. IV. and V. 3s. 6d. Or the five Books in separate vols. 1s. 6d. each.
Lucan. The Pharsalia. By C. E. Haskins, M.A., and W. E. Heitland, M.A. Demy 8vo. 14s.
Lucretius. With Commentary by H. A. J. Munro. 4th Edition. Vols. I. and II. Introduction, Text, and Notes. 18s. Vol. III. Translation. 6s.
Ovid. P. Ovidii Nasonis Heroides XIV. By A. Palmer, M.A. 8vo. 6s.
——— P. Ovidii Nasonis Ars Amatoria et Amores. By the Rev. H. Williams, M.A. 3s. 6d.
——— Metamorphoses. Book XIII. By Chas. Haines Keene, M.A. 2s. 6d.
——— Epistolarum ex Ponto Liber Primus. By C.H.Keene,M.A. 3s.
Propertius. Sex Aurelii Propertii Carmina. By F. A. Paley, M.A., LL.D. 8vo. Cloth, 5s.
——— Sex Propertii Elegiarum. Libri IV. Recensuit A. Palmer, Collegii Sacrosanctæ et Individuæ Trinitatis juxta Dublinum Socius. Fcap. 8vo. 3s. 6d.
Sophocles. The Oedipus Tyrannus. By B. H. Kennedy, D.D. Crown 8vo. 8s.
Thucydides. The History of the Peloponnesian War. By Richard Shilleto, M.A. Book I. 8vo. 6s. 6d. Book II. 8vo. 5s. 6d.

LOWER FORM SERIES.
With Notes and Vocabularies.

Eclogæ Latinæ; or, First Latin Reading-Book, with English Notes and a Dictionary. By the late Rev. P. Frost, M.A. New Edition. Fcap. 8vo. 1s. 6d.
Latin Vocabularies for Repetition. By A. M. M. Stedman, M.A. 2nd Edition, revised. Fcap. 8vo. 1s. 6d.
Easy Latin Passages for Unseen Translation. By A. M. M. Stedman, M.A. Fcap. 8vo. 1s. 6d.
Virgil's Æneid. Book I. Abridged from Conington's Edition by Rev. J. G. Sheppard, D.C.L. With Vocabulary by W. F. R. Shilleto. 1s. 6d. [*Now ready.*
Cæsar de Bello Gallico. Books I., II. and III. With Notes by George Long, M.A., and Vocabulary by W. F. R. Shilleto. 1s. 6d. each.
Tales for Latin Prose Composition. With Notes and Vocabulary. By G. H. Wells, M.A. 2s.
A Latin Verse-Book. An Introductory Work on Hexameters and Pentameters. By the late Rev. P. Frost, M.A. New Edition. Fcap. 8vo. 2s. Key (for Tutors only), 5s.
Analecta Græca Minora, with Introductory Sentences, English Notes, and a Dictionary. By the late Rev. P. Frost, M.A. New Edition. Fcap. 8vo. 2s.
Greek Testament Selections. 2nd Edition, enlarged, with Notes and Vocabulary. By A. M. M. Stedman, M.A. Fcap. 8vo. 2s. 6d.

LATIN AND GREEK CLASS-BOOKS.

(See also *Lower Form Series*.)

Faciliora. An Elementary Latin Book on a new principle. By the Rev. J. L. Seager, M.A. 2s. 6d.

First Latin Lessons. By A. M. M. Stedman. 1s.

Easy Latin Exercises, for Use with the Revised Latin Primer and Shorter Latin Primer. By A. M. M. Stedman, M.A. (Issued with the consent of the late Dr. Kennedy.) Crown 8vo. 2s. 6d.

Miscellaneous Latin Exercises. By A. M. M. Stedman, M.A. Fcap. 8vo. 1s. 6d.

A Latin Primer. By Rev. A. C. Clapin, M.A. 1s.

Auxilia Latina. A Series of Progressive Latin Exercises. By M. J. B. Baddeley, M.A. Fcap. 8vo. Part I. Accidence. 3rd Edition, revised. 2s. Part II. 4th Edition, revised. 2s. Key to Part II. 2s. 6d.

Scala Latina. Elementary Latin Exercises. By Rev. J. W. Davis, M.A. New Edition, with Vocabulary. Fcap. 8vo. 2s. 6d.

Passages for Translation into Latin Prose. By Prof. H. Nettleship, M.A. 3s. Key (for Tutors only), 4s. 6d.

Latin Prose Lessons. By Prof. Church, M.A. 9th Edition. Fcap. 8vo. 2s. 6d.

Analytical Latin Exercises. By C. P. Mason, B.A. 4th Edit. Part I., 1s. 6d. Part II., 2s. 6d.

By T. COLLINS, M.A., Head Master of the Latin School, Newport, Salop.

Latin Exercises and Grammar Papers. 6th Edit. Fcap. 8vo. 2s. 6d.

Unseen Papers in Latin Prose and Verse. With Examination Questions. 4th Edition. Fcap. 8vo. 2s. 6d.

—— **in Greek Prose and Verse.** With Examination Questions. 3rd Edition. Fcap. 8vo. 3s.

Easy Translations from Nepos, Cæsar, Cicero, Livy, &c., for Retranslation into Latin. With Notes. 2s.

By A. M. M. STEDMAN, M.A., Wadham College, Oxford.

Latin Examination Papers in Grammar and Idiom. 2nd Edition. Crown 8vo. 2s. 6d. Key (for Tutors and Private Students only), 6s.

Greek Examination Papers in Grammar and Idiom. 2s. 6d.

By the REV. P. FROST, M.A., St. John's College, Cambridge.

Materials for Latin Prose Composition. By the late Rev. P. Frost, M.A. New Edition. Fcap. 8vo. 2s. Key (for Tutors only), 4s.

Materials for Greek Prose Composition. New Edit. Fcap. 8vo. 2s. 6d. Key (for Tutors only), 5s.

Florilegium Poeticum. Elegiac Extracts from Ovid and Tibullus. New Edition. With Notes. Fcap. 8vo. 2s.

By H. A. HOLDEN, LL.D., formerly Fellow of Trinity Coll., Camb.

Foliorum Silvula. Part I. Passages for Translation into Latin Elegiac and Heroic Verse. 10th Edition. Post 8vo. 7s. 6d.

—— Part II. Select Passages for Translation into Latin Lyric and Comic Iambic Verse. 3rd Edition. Post 8vo. 5s.

Folia Silvulæ, sive Eclogæ Poetarum Anglicorum in Latinum et Græcum conversæ. 8vo. Vol. II. 4s. 6d.

Foliorum Centuriæ. Select Passages for Translation into Latin and Greek Prose. 10th Edition. Post 8vo. 8s.

Educational Works. 7

Scala Græca: a Series of Elementary Greek Exercises. By Rev. J. W. Davis, M.A., and R. W. Baddeley, M.A. 3rd Edition. Fcap. 8vo. 2s. 6d.
Greek Verse Composition. By G. Preston, M.A. 5th Edition. Crown 8vo. 4s. 6d.
Greek Particles and their Combinations according to Attic Usage. A Short Treatise. By F. A. Paley, M.A., LL.D. 2s. 6d.
Rudiments of Attic Construction and Idiom. By the Rev. W. C. Compton, M.A., Assistant Master at Uppingham School. 3s.
Anthologia Græca. A Selection of Choice Greek Poetry, with Notes. By F. St. John Thackeray. 4th and Cheaper Edition. 16mo. 4s. 6d.
Anthologia Latina. A Selection of Choice Latin Poetry, from Nævius to Boëthius, with Notes. By Rev. F. St. John Thackeray. Revised and Cheaper Edition. 16mo. 4s. 6d.

TRANSLATIONS, SELECTIONS, &c.

*** Many of the following books are well adapted for School Prizes.

Aeschylus. Translated into English Prose by F. A. Paley, M.A., LL.D. 2nd Edition. 8vo. 7s. 6d.
—— Translated into English Verse by Anna Swanwick. 4th Edition. Post 8vo. 5s.
Horace. The Odes and Carmen Sæculare. In English Verse by J. Conington, M.A. 10th edition. Fcap. 8vo. 5s. 6d.
—— The Satires and Epistles. In English Verse by J. Conington, M.A. 7th edition. 6s. 6d.
—— Odes. Englished and Imitated by various hands. 1s. 6d.
Plato. Gorgias. Translated by E. M. Cope, M.A. 8vo. 2nd Ed. 7s.
—— Philebus. Trans. by F. A. Paley, M.A., LL.D. Sm. 8vo. 4s.
—— Theætetus. Trans. by F. A. Paley, M.A., LL.D. Sm. 8vo. 4s.
—— Analysis and Index of the Dialogues. By Dr. Day. Post 8vo. 5s.
Sophocles. Oedipus Tyrannus. By Dr. Kennedy. 1s.
—— The Dramas of. Rendered into English Verse by Sir George Young, Bart., M.A. 8vo. 12s. 6d.
Theocritus. In English Verse, by C. S. Calverley, M.A. New Edition, revised. Crown 8vo. 7s. 6d.
Translations into English and Latin. By C. S. Calverley, M.A. Post 8vo. 7s. 6d.
Translations into English, Latin, and Greek. By R. C. Jebb, Litt. D., H. Jackson, Litt.D., and W. E. Currey, M.A. Second Edition. 8s.
Extracts for Translation. By R. C. Jebb, Litt. D., H. Jackson, Litt.D., and W. E. Currey, M.A. 4s. 6d.
Between Whiles. Translations by Rev. B. H. Kennedy, D.D. 2nd Edition, revised. Crown 8vo. 5s.
Sabrinae Corolla in Hortulis Regiae Scholae Salopiensis Contexuerunt Tres Viri Floribus Legendis. Fourth Edition, thoroughly Revised and Rearranged. With many new Pieces and an Introduction.
[*Ready immediately.*

REFERENCE VOLUMES.

A Latin Grammar. By Albert Harkness. Post 8vo. 6s.
—— By T. H. Key, M.A. 6th Thousand. Post 8vo. 8s.
A Short Latin Grammar for Schools. By T. H. Key, M.A. F.R.S. 16th Edition. Post 8vo. 3s. 6d.

A Guide to the Choice of Classical Books. By J. B. Mayor, M.A.
3rd Edition, with a Supplementary List. Crown 8vo. 4s. 6d. Supplementary List separately, 1s. 6d.
The Theatre of the Greeks. By J. W. Donaldson, D.D. 8th Edition. Post 8vo. 5s.
Keightley's Mythology of Greece and Italy. 4th Edition. 5s.

CLASSICAL TABLES.

Latin Accidence. By the Rev. P. Frost, M.A. 1s.
Latin Versification. 1s.
Notabilia Quædam; or the Principal Tenses of most of the Irregular Greek Verbs and Elementary Greek, Latin, and French Construction. New Edition. 1s.
Richmond Rules for the Ovidian Distich, &c. By J. Tate, M.A. 1s.
The Principles of Latin Syntax. 1s.
Greek Verbs. A Catalogue of Verbs, Irregular and Defective. By J. S. Baird, T.C.D. 8th Edition. 2s. 6d.
Greek Accents (Notes on). By A. Barry, D.D. New Edition. 1s.
Homeric Dialect. Its Leading Forms and Peculiarities. By J. S. Baird, T.C.D. New Edition, by W. G. Rutherford, LL.D. 1s.
Greek Accidence. By the Rev. P. Frost, M.A. New Edition. 1s.

CAMBRIDGE MATHEMATICAL SERIES.

Arithmetic for Schools. By C. Pendlebury, M.A. 3rd Edition, revised and stereotyped, with or without answers, 4s. 6d. Or in two parts, 2s. 6d. each.
EXAMPLES (nearly 8000), without answers, in a separate vol. 3s.
In use at St. Paul's, Winchester, Charterhouse, Merchant Taylors', Christ's Hospital, Sherborne, Shrewsbury, and at many other Schools and Colleges.
Algebra. Choice and Chance. By W. A. Whitworth, M.A. 4th Edition. 6s.
Euclid. Books I.-VI. and part of Books XI. and XII. By H. Deighton. 4s. 6d. Key (for Tutors only), 5s. Books I. and II., 2s.
Euclid. Exercises on Euclid and in Modern Geometry. By J. McDowell, M.A. 3rd Edition. 6s.
Trigonometry. Plane. By Rev. T. Vyvyan, M.A. 3rd Edit. 3s. 6d.
Geometrical Conic Sections. By H. G. Willis, M.A. Manchester Grammar School. 5s.
Conics. The Elementary Geometry of. 6th Edition, revised and enlarged. By C. Taylor, D.D. 4s. 6d.
Solid Geometry. By W. S. Aldis, M.A. 4th Edit. revised. 6s.
Geometrical Optics. By W. S. Aldis, M.A. 3rd Edition. 4s.
Rigid Dynamics. By W. S. Aldis, M.A. 4s.
Elementary Dynamics. By W. Garnett, M.A., D.C.L. 5th Ed. 6s.
Dynamics. A Treatise on. By W. H. Besant, Sc.D., F.R.S. 7s. 6d.
Heat. An Elementary Treatise. By W. Garnett, M.A., D.C.L. 5th Edition, revised and enlarged. 4s. 6d.
Elementary Physics. Examples in. By W. Gallatly, M.A. 4s.
Hydromechanics. By W. H. Besant, Sc.D., F.R.S. 4th Edition. Part I. Hydrostatics. 5s.
Mathematical Examples. By J. M. Dyer, M.A., Eton College, and R. Prowde Smith, M.A., Cheltenham College. 6s.
Mechanics. Problems in Elementary. By W. Walton, M.A. 6s.

CAMBRIDGE SCHOOL AND COLLEGE TEXT-BOOKS.
A Series of Elementary Treatises for the use of Students.

Arithmetic. By Rev. C. Elsee, M.A. Fcap. 8vo. 13th Edit. 3s. 6d.

―――― By A. Wrigley, M.A. 3s. 6d.

―――― A Progressive Course of Examples. With Answers. By J. Watson, M.A. 7th Edition, revised. By W. P. Goudie, B.A. 2s. 6d.

Algebra. By the Rev. C. Elsee, M.A. 7th Edit. 4s.

―――― Progressive Course of Examples. By Rev. W. F. M'Michael, M.A., and R. Prowde Smith, M.A. 4th Edition. 3s. 6d. With Answers. 4s. 6d.

Plane Astronomy, An Introduction to. By P. T. Main, M.A. 5th Edition. 4s.

Conic Sections treated Geometrically. By W. H. Besant, Sc.D. 7th Edition. 4s. 6d. Solution to the Examples. 4s.

―――― Enunciations and Figures Separately. 1s. 6d.

Statics, Elementary. By Rev. H. Goodwin, D.D. 2nd Edit. 3s.

Hydrostatics, Elementary. By W. H. Besant, Sc.D. 13th Edit. 4s.

Mensuration, An Elementary Treatise on. By B.T. Moore, M.A. 3s. 6d.

Newton's Principia, The First Three Sections of, with an Appendix; and the Ninth and Eleventh Sections. By J. H. Evans, M.A. 5th Edition, by P. T. Main, M.A. 4s.

Analytical Geometry for Schools. By T. G. Vyvyan. 5th Edit. 4s. 6d.

Greek Testament, Companion to the. By A. C. Barrett, M.A. 5th Edition, revised. Fcap. 8vo. 5s.

Book of Common Prayer, An Historical and Explanatory Treatise on the. By W. G. Humphry, B.D. 6th Edition. Fcap. 8vo. 2s. 6d.

Music, Text-book of. By Professor H. C. Banister. 14th Edition, revised. 5s.

―――― Concise History of. By Rev. H. G. Bonavia Hunt, Mus. Doc. Dublin. 10th Edition revised. 3s. 6d.

ARITHMETIC AND ALGEBRA.
See also the two foregoing Series.

Arithmetic, Examination Papers in. Consisting of 140 papers, each containing 7 questions. 357 more difficult problems follow. A collection of recent Public Examination Papers are appended. By C. Pendlebury, M.A. 2s. 6d. Key, for Masters only, 5s.

Algebra, Examination Papers in. *Preparing.*

Graduated Exercises in Addition (Simple and Compound). By W. S. Beard, C. S. Dept. Rochester Mathematical School. 1s.
The Answers sent free to Masters only.
For Candidates for Commercial Certificates and Civil Service Exams.

BOOK-KEEPING.

Book-keeping Papers, set at various Public Examinations. Collected and Written by J. T. Medhurst, Lecturer on Book-keeping in the City of London College. 3s.

GEOMETRY AND EUCLID.

Euclid. Books I.-VI. and part of XI. and XII. A New Translation. By H. Deighton. Books I. and II. separately, 2s. (See p. 8.)
—— The Definitions of, with Explanations and Exercises, and an Appendix of Exercises on the First Book. By R. Webb, M.A. Crown 8vo. 1s. 6d.
—— Book I. With Notes and Exercises for the use of Preparatory Schools, &c. By Braithwaite Arnett, M.A. 8vo. 4s. 6d.
—— The First Two Books explained to Beginners. By C. P. Mason, B.A. 2nd Edition. Fcap. 8vo. 2s. 6d.
The Enunciations and Figures to Euclid's Elements. By Rev. J. Brasse, D.D. New Edition. Fcap. 8vo. 1s. Without the Figures, 6d.
Exercises on Euclid and in Modern Geometry. By J. McDowell, B.A. Crown 8vo. 3rd Edition revised. 6s.
Geometrical Conic Sections. By H. G. Willis, M.A. (See p. 8.)
Geometrical Conic Sections. By W. H. Besant, D.Sc. (See p. 9.)
Elementary Geometry of Conics. By C. Taylor, D.D. (See p. 8.)
An Introduction to Ancient and Modern Geometry of Conics. By C. Taylor, D.D., Master of St. John's Coll., Camb. 8vo. 15s.
Solutions of Geometrical Problems, proposed at St. John's College from 1830 to 1846. By T. Gaskin, M.A. 8vo. 12s.

TRIGONOMETRY.

Trigonometry, Introduction to Plane. By Rev. T. G. Vyvyan, Charterhouse. 3rd Edition. Cr. 8vo. 3s. 6d.
An Elementary Treatise on Mensuration. By B. T. Moore, M.A. 3s. 6d.
Trigonometry, Examination Papers in. By G. H. Ward, M.A., Assistant Master at St. Paul's School. Crown 8vo. 2s. 6d.

ANALYTICAL GEOMETRY AND DIFFERENTIAL CALCULUS.

An Introduction to Analytical Plane Geometry. By W. P. Turnbull, M.A. 8vo. 12s.
Problems on the Principles of Plane Co-ordinate Geometry. By W. Walton, M.A. 8vo. 16s.
Trilinear Co-ordinates, and Modern Analytical Geometry of Two Dimensions. By W. A. Whitworth, M.A. 8vo. 16s.
An Elementary Treatise on Solid Geometry. By W. S. Aldis, M.A. 4th Edition revised. Cr. 8vo. 6s.
Elliptic Functions, Elementary Treatise on. By A. Cayley, Sc.D. Professor of Pure Mathematics at Cambridge University. Demy 8vo. 15s.

MECHANICS & NATURAL PHILOSOPHY.

Statics, Elementary. By H. Goodwin, D.D. Fcap. 8vo. 2nd Edition. 3s.

Dynamics. A Treatise on Elementary. By W. Garnett, M.A., D.C.L. 5th Edition. Crown 8vo. 6s.

Dynamics. Rigid. By W. S. Aldis, M.A. 4s.

Dynamics. A Treatise on. By W. H. Besant, Sc.D., F.R.S. 7s. 6d.

Elementary Mechanics, Problems in. By W. Walton, M.A. New Edition. Crown 8vo. 6s.

Theoretical Mechanics, Problems in. By W. Walton, M.A. 3rd Edition. Demy 8vo. 16s.

Hydrostatics. By W. H. Besant, Sc.D. Fcap. 8vo. 13th Edition. 4s.

Hydromechanics, A Treatise on. By W. H. Besant, Sc.D., F.R.S. 8vo. 4th Edition, revised. Part I. Hydrostatics. 5s.

Hydrodynamics, A Treatise on. Vol. I. 10s. 6d.; Vol. II. 12s. 6d. A. B. Basset, M.A.

Optics. Geometrical. By W. S. Aldis, M.A. Crown 8vo. 3rd Edition. 4s.

Double Refraction, A Chapter on Fresnel's Theory of. By W. S. Aldis, M.A. 8vo. 2s.

Heat, An Elementary Treatise on. By W. Garnett, M.A., D.C.L. Crown 8vo. 5th Edition. 4s. 6d.

Elementary Physics. By W. Gallatly, M.A., Asst. Examr. at London University. 4s.

Newton's Principia, The First Three Sections of, with an Appendix; and the Ninth and Eleventh Sections. By J. H. Evans, M.A. 5th Edition. Edited by P. T. Main, M.A. 4s.

Astronomy, An Introduction to Plane. By P. T. Main, M.A. Fcap. 8vo. cloth. 5th Edition. 4s.

—— **Practical and Spherical.** By R. Main, M.A. 8vo. 14s.

Mathematical Examples. Pure and Mixed. By J. M. Dyer, M.A., and R. Prowde Smith, M.A. 6s.

Pure Mathematics and Natural Philosophy, A Compendium of Facts and Formulæ in. By G. R. Smalley. 2nd Edition, revised by J. McDowell, M.A. Fcap. 8vo. 3s. 6d.

Elementary Mathematical Formulæ. By the Rev. T. W. Openshaw, M.A. 1s. 6d.

Elementary Course of Mathematics. By H. Goodwin, D.D. 6th Edition. 8vo. 16s.

Problems and Examples, adapted to the 'Elementary Course of Mathematics.' 3rd Edition. 8vo. 5s.

Solutions of Goodwin's Collection of Problems and Examples. By W. W. Hutt, M.A. 3rd Edition, revised and enlarged. 8vo. 9s.

A Collection of Examples and Problems in Arithmetic, Algebra, Geometry, Logarithms, Trigonometry, Conic Sections, Mechanics, &c., with Answers. By Rev. A. Wrigley. 20th Thousand. 8s. 6d. Key. 10s 6d

Science Examination Papers. Part I. Inorganic Chemistry. By R. E. Steel, M.A., F.C.S., Bradford Grammar School. Crown 8vo. 2s. 6d.

TECHNOLOGICAL HANDBOOKS.

Edited by H. TRUEMAN WOOD, Secretary of the Society of Arts.

Dyeing and Tissue Printing. By W. Crookes, F.R.S. 5s.

Glass Manufacture. By Henry Chance, M.A.; H. J. Powell, B.A.; and H. G. Harris. 3s. 6d.

Cotton Spinning. By Richard Marsden, of Manchester. 3rd Edition, revised. 6s. 6d.

Chemistry of Coal-Tar Colours. By Prof. Benedikt, and Dr. Knecht of Bradford Technical College. 2nd Edition, enlarged. 6s. 6d.

Woollen and Worsted Cloth Manufacture. By Roberts Beaumont, Professor at Yorkshire College, Leeds. 7s. 6d.

Cotton Weaving. By R. Marsden. [*In the press.*

Colour in Woven Design. By Roberts Beaumont. [*In the press.*

Bookbinding. By Zaehnsdorf. [*Preparing.*

Others in preparation.

HISTORY, TOPOGRAPHY, &c.

Rome and the Campagna. By R. Burn, M.A. With 85 Engravings and 26 Maps and Plans. With Appendix. 4to. 21s.

Old Rome. A Handbook for Travellers. By R. Burn, M.A. With Maps and Plans. Demy 8vo. 5s.

Modern Europe. By Dr. T. H. Dyer. 2nd Edition, revised and continued. 5 vols. Demy 8vo. 2l. 12s. 6d.

The History of the Kings of Rome. By Dr. T. H. Dyer. 8vo. 5s.

The History of Pompeii: its Buildings and Antiquities. By T. H. Dyer. 3rd Edition, brought down to 1874. Post 8vo. 7s. 6d.

The City of Rome: its History and Monuments. 2nd Edition, revised by T. H. Dyer. 5s.

Ancient Athens: its History, Topography, and Remains. By T. H. Dyer. Super-royal 8vo. Cloth. 7s. 6d.

The Decline of the Roman Republic. By G. Long. 5 vols. 8vo. 5s. each.

Historical Maps of England. By C. H. Pearson. Folio. 3rd Edition revised. 31s. 6d.

History of England, 1800-46. By Harriet Martineau, with new and copious Index. 5 vols. 3s. 6d. each.

A Practical Synopsis of English History. By A. Bowes. 9th Edition, revised. 8vo. 1s.

Lives of the Queens of England. By A. Strickland. Library Edition, 8 vols. 7s. 6d. each. Cheaper Edition, 6 vols. 5s. each. Abridged Edition, 1 vol. 6s. 6d. Mary Queen of Scots, 2 vols. 5s. each. Tudor and Stuart Princesses, 5s.

Educational Works. 13

Eginhard's Life of Karl the Great (Charlemagne). Translated, with Notes, by W. Glaister, M.A., B.C.L. Crown 8vo. 4s. 6d.

The Elements of General History. By Prof. Tytler. New Edition, brought down to 1874. Small Post 8vo. 3s. 6d.

History and Geography Examination Papers. Compiled by C. H. Spence, M.A., Clifton College. Crown 8vo. 2s. 6d.

PHILOLOGY.

WEBSTER'S DICTIONARY OF THE ENGLISH LANGUAGE. With Dr. Mahn's Etymology. 1 vol. 1628 pages, 3000 Illustrations. 21s.; half calf, 30s.; calf or half russia, 31s. 6d.; russia, 2l. With Appendices and 70 additional pages of Illustrations, 1919 pages, 31s. 6d.; half calf, 2l.; calf or half russia, 2l. 2s.; russia, 2l. 10s.

'THE BEST PRACTICAL ENGLISH DICTIONARY EXTANT.'—*Quarterly Review*, 1873.

Prospectuses, with specimen pages, post free on application.

Richardson's Philological Dictionary of the English Language. Combining Explanation with Etymology, and copiously illustrated by Quotations from the best Authorities. With a Supplement. 2 vols. 4to. 4l. 14s. 6d. Supplement separately. 4to. 12s.

Brief History of the English Language. By Prof. James Hadley, LL.D., Yale College. Fcap. 8vo. 1s.

The Elements of the English Language. By E. Adams, Ph.D. 21st Edition. Post 8vo. 4s. 6d.

Philological Essays. By T. H. Key, M.A., F.R.S. 8vo. 10s. 6d.

Synonyms and Antonyms of the English Language. By Archdeacon Smith. 2nd Edition. Post 8vo. 5s.

Synonyms Discriminated. By Archdeacon Smith. Demy 8vo. 2nd Edition revised. 14s.

Bible English. Chapters on Words and Phrases in the Bible and Prayer Book. By Rev. T. L. O. Davies. 2nd Edition revised, in the press.

The Queen's English. A Manual of Idiom and Usage. By the late Dean Alford. 6th Edition. Fcap. 8vo. 1s. sewed. 1s. 6d. cloth.

A History of English Rhythms. By Edwin Guest, M.A., D.C.L. LL.D. New Edition, by Professor W. W. Skeat. Demy 8vo. 18s.

Elements of Comparative Grammar and Philology. For Use in Schools. By A. C. Price, M.A., Assistant Master at Leeds Grammar School. Crown 8vo. 2s. 6d.

Questions for Examination in English Literature. By Prof. W. W. Skeat. 2nd Edition, revised. 2s. 6d.

A Syriac Grammar. By G. Phillips, D.D. 3rd Edition, enlarged. 8vo. 7s. 6d.

14 *George Bell and Sons'*

DIVINITY, MORAL PHILOSOPHY, &c.

BY THE REV. F. H. SCRIVENER, A.M., LL.D., D.C.L.

Novum Testamentum Græce. Editio major. Being an enlarged Edition, containing the Readings of Westcott and Hort, and those adopted by the Revisers, &c. 7s. 6d. *For other Editions see page 3.*

A Plain Introduction to the Criticism of the New Testament. With Forty Facsimiles from Ancient Manuscripts. 3rd Edition. 8vo. 18s.

Six Lectures on the Text of the New Testament. For English Readers. Crown 8vo. 6s.

Codex Bezæ Cantabrigiensis. 4to. 10s. 6d.

The New Testament for English Readers. By the late H. Alford, D.D. Vol. I. Part I. 3rd Edit. 12s. Vol. I. Part II. 2nd Edit. 10s. 6d. Vol. II. Part I. 2nd Edit. 16s. Vol. II. Part II. 2nd Edit. 16s.

The Greek Testament. By the late H. Alford, D.D. Vol. I. 7th Edit. 1l. 8s. Vol. II. 8th Edit. 1l. 4s. Vol. III. 10th Edit. 18s. Vol. IV. Part I. 5th Edit. 18s. Vol. IV. Part II. 10th Edit. 14s. Vol. IV. 1l. 12s.

Companion to the Greek Testament. By A. C. Barrett, M.A. 5th Edition, revised. Fcap. 8vo. 5s.

Guide to the Textual Criticism of the New Testament. By Rev. E. Miller, M.A. Crown 8vo. 4s.

The Book of Psalms. A New Translation, with Introductions, &c. By the Very Rev. J. J. Stewart Perowne, D.D. 8vo. Vol. I. 6th Edition, 18s. Vol. II. 6th Edit. 16s.

—— Abridged for Schools. 6th Edition. Crown 8vo. 10s. 6d.

History of the Articles of Religion. By C. H. Hardwick. 3rd Edition. Post 8vo. 5s.

History of the Creeds. By J. R. Lumby, DD. 3rd Edition. Crown 8vo. 7s. 6d.

Pearson on the Creed. Carefully printed from an early edition. With Analysis and Index by E. Walford, M.A. Post 8vo. 5s.

Liturgies and Offices of the Church, for the Use of English Readers, in Illustration of the Book of Common Prayer. By the Rev. Edward Burbidge, M.A. Crown 8vo. 9s.

An Historical and Explanatory Treatise on the Book of Common Prayer By Rev. W. G. Humphry, B.D. 6th Edition, enlarged. Small Post 8vo. 2s. 6d.; Cheap Edition, 1s.

A Commentary on the Gospels, Epistles, and Acts of the Apostles. By Rev. W. Denton, A.M. New Edition. 7 vols. 8vo. 9s. each.

Notes on the Catechism. By Rt. Rev. Bishop Barry. 8th Edit. Fcap. 2s.

The Winton Church Catechist. Questions and Answers on the Teaching of the Church Catechism. By the late Rev. J. S. B. Monsell, LL.D. 4th Edition. Cloth, 3s.; or in Four Parts, sewed.

The Church Teacher's Manual of Christian Instruction. By Rev. M. F. Sadler. 38th Thousand. 2s. 6d.

Educational Works. 15

FOREIGN CLASSICS.

A Series for use in Schools, with English Notes, grammatical and explanatory, and renderings of difficult idiomatic expressions. Fcap. 8vo.

Schiller's Wallenstein. By Dr. A. Buchheim. 5th Edit. 5s.
Or the Lager and Piccolomini, 2s. 6d. Wallenstein's Tod, 2s. 6d.
——— **Maid of Orleans.** By Dr. W. Wagner. 2nd Edit. 1s. 6d.
——— **Maria Stuart.** By V. Kastner. 2nd Edition. 1s. 6d.
Goethe's Hermann and Dorothea. By E. Bell, M.A., and E. Wölfel. 1s. 6d.
German Ballads, from Uhland, Goethe, and Schiller. By C. L. Bielefeld. 3rd Edition. 1s. 6d.
Charles XII., par Voltaire. By L. Direy. 7th Edition. 1s. 6d.
Aventures de Télémaque, par Fénélon. By C. J. Delille. 4th Edition. 2s. 6d.
Select Fables of La Fontaine. By F. E. A. Gasc. 18th Edit. 1s. 6d.
Picciola, by X. B. Saintine. By Dr. Dubuc. 15th Thousand. 1s. 6d.
Lamartine's Le Tailleur de Pierres de Saint-Point. By J. Boïelle, 4th Thousand. Fcap. 8vo. 1s. 6d.

Italian Primer. By Rev. A. C. Clapin, M.A. Fcap. 8vo. 1s.

FRENCH CLASS-BOOKS.

French Grammar for Public Schools. By Rev. A. C. Clapin, M.A. Fcap. 8vo. 12th Edition, revised. 2s. 6d.
French Primer. By Rev. A. C. Clapin, M.A. Fcap. 8vo. 8th Ed. 1s.
Primer of French Philology. By Rev. A. C. Clapin. Fcap. 8vo. 4th Edit. 1s.
Le Nouveau Trésor; or, French Student's Companion. By M. E. S. 18th Edition. Fcap. 8vo. 1s. 6d.
French Examination Papers in Miscellaneous Grammar and Idioms. Compiled by A. M. M. Stedman, M.A. 4th Edition. Crown 8vo. 2s. 6d.
  Key to the above. By G. A. Schrumpf, Univ. of France. Crown 8vo. 5s. (For Teachers or Private Students only.)
Manual of French Prosody. By Arthur Gosset, M.A. Crown 8vo. 3s.
Lexicon of Conversational French. By A. Holloway. 3rd Edition. Crown 8vo. 4s.

PROF. A. BARRÈRE'S FRENCH COURSE.

Elements of French Grammar and First Steps in Idiom. Crown 8vo. 2s.
Precis of Comparative French Grammar. 2nd Edition. Crown 8vo. 3s. 6d.
Junior Graduated French Course. Crown 8vo. 1s. 6d.

F. E. A. GASC'S FRENCH COURSE.

First French Book. Fcap. 8vo. 106th Thousand. 1s.
Second French Book. 47th Thousand. Fcap. 8vo. 1s. 6d.
Key to First and Second French Books. 5th Edit. Fcp. 8vo. 3s. 6d.
French Fables for Beginners, in Prose, with Index. 16th Thousand.
  12mo. 1s. 6d.
Select Fables of La Fontaine. 18th Thousand. Fcap. 8vo. 1s. 6d.
Histoires Amusantes et Instructives. With Notes. 16th Thousand. Fcap. 8vo. 2s.
Practical Guide to Modern French Conversation. 17th Thousand. Fcap. 8vo. 1s. 6d.
French Poetry for the Young. With Notes. 5th Ed. Fcp. 8vo. 8s.
Materials for French Prose Composition; or, Selections from the best English Prose Writers. 19th Thous. Fcap. 8vo. 3s. Key, 6s.
Prosateurs Contemporains. With Notes. 10th Edition, revised. 12mo. 3s. 6d.
Le Petit Compagnon; a French Talk-Book for Little Children. 12th Thousand. 16mo. 1s 6d.
An Improved Modern Pocket Dictionary of the French and English Languages. 45th Thousand. 16mo. 2s. 6d.
Modern French-English and English-French Dictionary. 4th Edition, revised, with new supplements. 10s. 6d.
The A B C Tourist's French Interpreter of all Immediate Wants. By F. E. A. Gasc. 1s.

MODERN FRENCH AUTHORS.

Edited, with Introductions and Notes, by JAMES BOÏELLE, Senior French Master at Dulwich College.

Daudet's La Belle Nivernaise. 2s. 6d. *For Beginners.*
Hugo's Bug Jargal. 3s. *For Advanced Students.*

GOMBERT'S FRENCH DRAMA.

Being a Selection of the best Tragedies and Comedies of Molière, Racine, Corneille, and Voltaire. With Arguments and Notes by A. Gombert. New Edition, revised by F. E. A. Gasc. Fcap. 8vo. 1s. each; sewed, 6d. CONTENTS.

MOLIÈRE:—Le Misanthrope. L'Avare. Le Bourgeois Gentilhomme. Le Tartuffe. Le Malade Imaginaire. Les Femmes Savantes. Les Fourberies de Scapin. Les Précieuses Ridicules. L'Ecole des Femmes. L'Ecole des Maris. Le Médecin malgré Lui.
RACINE:—Phédre. Esther. Athalie. Iphigénie. Les Plaidours. La Thébaïde; ou, Les Frères Ennemis. Andromaque. Britannicus.
P. CORNEILLE:—Le Cid. Horace. Cinna. Polyeucte.
VOLTAIRE:—Zaïre.

GERMAN CLASS-BOOKS.

Materials for German Prose Composition. By Dr. Buchheim. 12th Edition, thoroughly revised. Fcap. 4s. 6d. Key, Parts I. and II., 3s. Parts III. and IV., 4s.
German Conversation Grammar. By I. Sydow. 2nd Edition.
  Book I. Etymology. 2s. 6d. Book II. Syntax. 1s. 6d.

Wortfolge, or Rules and Exercises on the Order of Words in
German Sentences. By Dr. F. Stock. 1s. 6d.
A German Grammar for Public Schools. By the Rev. A. C.
Clapin and F. Holl Müller. 5th Edition. Fcap. 2s. 6d.
A German Primer, with Exercises. By Rev. A. C. Clapin. 1s.
Kotzebue's Der Gefangene. With Notes by Dr. W. Stromberg. 1s.
German Examination Papers in Grammar and Idiom. By
R. J. Morich. 2s. 6d. Key for Tutors only, 5s.
By FRZ. LANGE, Ph.D., Professor R.M.A., Woolwich, Examiner
in German to the Coll. of Preceptors, and also at the
Victoria University, Manchester.
A Concise German Grammar. In Three Parts. Part I. Elementary. 2s. Part II. Intermediate. 1s. 6d. Part III. Advanced, 3s. 6d.
German Examination Course. Elementary, 2s. Intermediate, 2s.
Advanced, 1s. 6d.
German Reader. Elementary. 1s. 6d. Advanced (*in the press*).

MODERN GERMAN SCHOOL CLASSICS.
Small Crown 8vo.
Hey's Fabeln Für Kinder. Edited by Prof. F. Lange, Ph.D. 1s. 6d.
Benedix's Dr. Wespe. Edited by F. Lange, Ph.D. 2s. 6d.
Hoffman's Meister Martin, der Küfner. By Prof. F. Lange, Ph.D.
1s. 6d.
Heyse's Hans Lange. By A. A. Macdonell, M.A., Ph.D. 2s.
Auerbach's Auf Wache, and Roquette's Der Gefrorene Kuss.
By A. A. Macdonell, M.A. 2s.
Moser's Der Bibliothekar. By Prof. F. Lange, Ph.D. 2s.
Ebers' Eine Frage. By F. Storr, B.A. 2s.
Freytag's Die Journalisten. By Prof. F. Lange, Ph.D. 2s. 6d.
Gutzkow's Zopf und Schwert. By Prof. F. Lange, Ph.D. 2s.
German Epic Tales. Edited by Kar lNeuhaus, Ph.D. 2s. 6d.

ENGLISH CLASS-BOOKS.
Comparative Grammar and Philology. By A. C. Price, M.A.,
Assistant Master at Leeds Grammar School. 2s. 6d.
The Elements of the English Language. By E. Adams, Ph.D.
22nd Edition. Post 8vo. 4s. 6d.
The Rudiments of English Grammar and Analysis. By
E. Adams, Ph.D. 17th Thousand. Fcap. 8vo. 1s.
A Concise System of Parsing. By L. E. Adams, B.A. 1s. 6d.
General Knowledge Examination Papers. Compiled by
A. M. M. Stedman, M.A. 2s. 6d.
Examples for Grammatical Analysis (Verse and Prose). Selected, &c., by F. Edwards. New edition. Cloth, 1s.
Notes on Shakespeare's Plays. By T. Duff Barnett, B.A.
MIDSUMMER NIGHT'S DREAM, 1s.; JULIUS CÆSAR, 1s.; HENRY V., 1s.;
TEMPEST, 1s.; MACBETH, 1s.; MERCHANT OF VENICE, 1s.; HAMLET, 1s.

By C. P. MASON, Fellow of Univ. Coll. London.

First Notions of Grammar for Young Learners. Fcap. 8vo. 47th Thousand. Cloth. 9d.

First Steps in English Grammar for Junior Classes. Demy 18mo. 46th Thousand. 1s.

Outlines of English Grammar for the Use of Junior Classes. 71st to 76th Thousand. Crown 8vo. 2s.

English Grammar, including the Principles of Grammatical Analysis. 31st Edition. 125th to 130th Thousand. Crown 8vo. 3s. 6d.

Practice and Help in the Analysis of Sentences. 2s.

A Shorter English Grammar, with copious Exercises. 34th to 38th Thousand. Crown 8vo. 3s. 6d.

English Grammar Practice, being the Exercises separately. 1s.

Code Standard Grammars. Parts I. and II., 2d. each. Parts III., IV., and V., 3d. each.

Notes of Lessons, their Preparation, &c. By José Rickard, Park Lane Board School, Leeds, and A. H. Taylor, Rodley Board School, Leeds. 2nd Edition. Crown 8vo. 2s. 6d.

A Syllabic System of Teaching to Read, combining the advantages of the 'Phonic' and the 'Look-and-Say' Systems. Crown 8vo. 1s.

Practical Hints on Teaching. By Rev. J. Menet, M.A. 6th Edit. revised. Crown 8vo. paper, 2s.

How to Earn the Merit Grant. A Manual of School Management. By H. Major, B.A., B.Sc. Part I. (3rd Edit.) Infant School, 3s. Part II. (2nd Edit. revised), 4s. Complete, 6s.

Test Lessons in Dictation. 4th Edition. Paper cover, 1s. 6d.

The Botanist's Pocket-Book. With a copious Index. By W. R. Hayward. 6th Edition, revised. Crown 8vo. cloth limp. 4s. 6d.

Experimental Chemistry, founded on the Work of Dr. Stöckhardt. By C. W. Heaton. Post 8vo. 5s.

Lectures on Musical Analysis. Sonata-form, Fugue, &c. By Prof. H. C. Banister. 2nd Edition, revised. 7s. 6d.

Helps' Course of Poetry, for Schools. A New Selection from the English Poets, carefully compiled and adapted to the several standards by E. A. Helps, one of H.M. Inspectors of Schools.

    Book I. Infants and Standards I. and II. 134 pp. small 8vo. 9d.
    Book II. Standards III. and IV. 224 pp. crown 8vo. 1s. 6d.
    Book III. Standards V., VI., and VII. 352 pp. post 8vo. 2s.
    Or in PARTS. Infants, 2d.; Standard I., 2d.; Standard II., 2d. Standard III., 4d.

Picture School-Books. In Simple Language, with numerous Illustrations. Royal 16mo.

The Infant's Primer. 3d.—School Primer. 6d.—School Reader. By J. Tilleard. 1s.—Poetry Book for Schools. 1s.—The Life of Joseph. 1s.—The Scripture Parables. By the Rev. J. E. Clarke. 1s.—The Scripture Miracles. By the Rev. J. E. Clarke. 1s.—The New Testament History. By the Rev. J. G. Wood, M.A. 1s.—The Old Testament History. By the Rev. J. G. Wood, M.A. 1s.—The Life of Martin Luther. By Sarah Crompton. 1s.

Educational Works. 19

BOOKS FOR YOUNG READERS.

A Series of Reading Books designed to facilitate the acquisition of the power of Reading by very young Children. In 11 vols. limp cloth, 6d. each.

Those with an asterisk have a Frontispiece or other Illustrations.

*The Old Boathouse. Bell and Fan; or, A Cold Dip.

*Tot and the Cat. A Bit of Cake. The Jay. The Black Hen's Nest. Tom and Ned. Mrs. Bee. } *Suitable*
*The Cat and the Hen. Sam and his Dog Redleg. } *for*
Bob and Tom Lee. A Wreck. } *Infants.*

*The New-born Lamb. The Rosewood Box. Poor Fan. Sheep Dog.

*The Two Parrots. A Tale of the Jubilee. By M. E. Wintle. 9 Illustrations.

*The Story of Three Monkeys.

*Story of a Cat. Told by Herself.

The Blind Boy. The Mute Girl. A New Tale of } *Suitable*
Babes in a Wood. } *for*
The Dey and the Knight. The New Bank Note. } *Standards*
The Royal Visit. A King's Walk on a Winter's Day. } *I. & II.*

*Queen Bee and Busy Bee.

*Gull's Crag.

*A First Book of Geography. By the Rev. C. A. Johns. Illustrated. Double size, 1s.

Syllabic Spelling. By C. Barton. In Two Parts. Infants, 3d. Standard I., 3d.

GEOGRAPHICAL SERIES. By M. J. BARRINGTON WARD, M.A. *With Illustrations.*

The Map and the Compass. A Reading-Book of Geography. For Standard I. New Edition, revised. 8d. cloth.

The Round World. A Reading-Book of Geography. For Standard II. 10d.

About England. A Reading Book of Geography for Standard III. [*In the press.*

The Child's Geography. For the Use of Schools and for Home Tuition. 6d.

The Child's Geography of England. With Introductory Exercises on the British Isles and Empire, with Questions. 2s. 6d. Without Questions, 2s.

Geography Examination Papers. (See History and Geography Papers, p. 12.)

BELL'S READING-BOOKS.
FOR SCHOOLS AND PAROCHIAL LIBRARIES.
Now Ready. Post 8vo. Strongly bound in cloth, 1s. each.

*Life of Columbus.
*Grimm's German Tales. (Selected.)
*Andersen's Danish Tales. Illustrated. (Selected.)
Great Englishmen. Short Lives for Young Children.
Great Englishwomen. Short Lives of.
Great Scotsmen. Short Lives of.

Suitable for Standards III. & IV.

*Masterman Ready. By Capt. Marryat. Illus. (Abgd.)
*Poor Jack. By Capt. Marryat, R.N. (Abridged.)

*Scott's Talisman. (Abridged.)
*Friends in Fur and Feathers. By Gwynfryn.
*Poor Jack. By Captain Marryat, R.N. Abgd.
Parables from Nature. (Selected.) By Mrs. Gatty.
Lamb's Tales from Shakespeare. (Selected.)
Edgeworth's Tales. (A Selection.)
*Gulliver's Travels. (Abridged.)
*Robinson Crusoe. Illustrated.
*Arabian Nights. (A Selection Rewritten.)

Standards IV. & V.

*Dickens's Little Nell. Abridged from the 'The Old Curiosity Shop.'
*The Vicar of Wakefield.
*Settlers in Canada. By Capt. Marryat. (Abridged.)
Marie: Glimpses of Life in France. By A. R. Ellis.
Poetry for Boys. Selected by D. Munro.
*Southey's Life of Nelson. (Abridged.)
*Life of the Duke of Wellington, with Maps and Plans.
*Sir Roger de Coverley and other Essays from the Spectator.
Tales of the Coast. By J. Runciman.

Standards V. VI. & VII.

* *These Volumes are Illustrated.*

Uniform with the Series, in limp cloth, 6d. each.

Shakespeare's Plays. Kemble's Reading Edition. With Explanatory Notes for School Use.
JULIUS CÆSAR. THE MERCHANT OF VENICE. KING JOHN.
HENRY THE FIFTH. MACBETH. AS YOU LIKE IT.

London: **GEORGE BELL & SONS**, York Str et, Covent Garden.

www.ingramcontent.com/pod-product-compliance
Lightning Source LLC
Chambersburg PA
CBHW022118290426
44112CB00008B/720